T4-AJW-916

With the compliments of

F. E. PEACOCK PUBLISHERS, INC.
401 WEST IRVING PARK ROAD
ITASCA, ILLINOIS 60143

Over There: European Reaction to
Americans in World War I

Primary Sources in American History

CONSULTING EDITOR
Grady McWhiney, Wayne State University

IMPERIALISTS VERSUS ANTI-IMPERIALISTS:
The Debate Over Expansionism in the 1890's
Richard E. Welch, Jr.

AMERICAN UTOPIANISM
Robert S. Fogarty

SLAVERY IN AMERICA: Theodore Weld's
American Slavery As It Is
Richard O. Curry and
Joanna Dunlap Cowden

OVER THERE

European

Reaction

To

Americans

In

World

War I

ROBERT C. WALTON

WAYNE STATE UNIVERSITY

F. E. PEACOCK PUBLISHERS, INC.

ITASCA, ILLINOIS 60143

JOHN W. CAUGHEY, Advisory Editor

To those on the other side
who died at the end
without hope

Table of Contents

Sources

Unpublished Sources

Bayrischen Hauptstaatsarchiv Abt. IV Kriegsarchiv, Munich: M.
Kr. 41, 1775, 1828–32.
Hauptstaatsarchiv, Stuttgart: Nachlass Conrad Haussmann,
1857–1922; Flugschriften Amerika im Weltkrieg, 6.
Hauptstaatsarchiv, Stuttgart, *Abt. Heeresarchiv: Persönliche Angelegenheiten des Württembergischen Kriegsministers. Berichte
des Militärbevollmächtigten beim grossen Hauptquartier und
des Stellvertretenden Militärbevollmächtigten in Berlin,*
1914–18.
Haus-, Hof- und Staatsarchiv, Vienna: PA XXXIII, 52 U.S.A.
Kriegsarchiv, Vienna: EvB.5622, 5784 (Nord-Amerika); Pk VIII,
1/1, 1/4, 1/8, 1/9.
Public Record Office:
    F.O. 371/var.
    F.O. 382/var.
    F.O. 395/var.
    W.O. 32/var.
    W.O. 106/var.
    W.O. 158/var.
    GFM 21/380

Published sources

*Les armées françaises dans la grande guerre, Ministère de la
guerre. Etat Major de l'armée. Service Historique,* 11 vols.
(Paris, 1922–39).
*Oesterreich-Ungarns letzter Krieg 1914–1918. Hr. vom Oesterr.
Bundeministerium für Heerwesen u. vom Kriegsarchive unter*

Leitung von E. v. Glaise—Horstenau, 8 vols. (Vienna, 1929-38).

Der Weltkrieg 1914-1918. Bearbeitet im Reichsarchiv und von der kriegsgeschichtlichen Forschungsanstalt des Heeres, 14 vols. (Berlin, 1925-1944).

Secondary sources

Cruttwell, C. R. M. F., *A History of the Great War, 1914-1918* (Oxford: At the Clarendon Press, 1934).

Delbrück, Hans, *Krieg und Politik,* 3 vols. (Berlin: Verlag von Georg Stilke, 1919).

Edmonds, Brigadier-General Sir James E., *A Short History of World War I* (Oxford: Oxford University Press, 1951).

Falls, Cyril, *The Great War* (New York: G. P. Putnam, 1959).

Jünger, Ernst, *Werke, Tagebücher* (Stuttgart: Ernst Klett, no date), I.

Janssen, Karl-Heinz, *Der Kanzler und der General. Die Führungs-krise um Bethmann Hollweg und Falkenhayn 1914-16* (Göttingen: Musterschmidt Verlag, 1967).

Janssen, Karl-Heinz, *Macht und Verblendung Kriegszielpolitik der deutschen Bundesstaaten 1914-18* (Göttingen: Musterschmidt Verlag, 1963).

Kielmansegg, Peter Graf, *Deutschland und der Erste Weltkrieg* (Frankfurt: Akademische Verlagsgesellschaft, 1968).

Liddell Hart, B. H.,*Through the Fog of War* (London: Faber and Faber, 1938)

Pitt, Barrie, *1918: The Last Act* (New York: Norton, 1964).

Ritter, Gerhard, *Staatskunst und Kriegshandwerk,* 4 vols. (Munich: Verlag R. Oldenbourg, 1958-68), Vol. IV.

Rössler, H. (ed.), *Weltwende, 1917* (Göttingen: Musterschmidt Verlag, 1965).

Smith, Daniel M., *The Great Departure: The United States and World War I* (New York: John Wiley and Sons, 1965).

Woodward, Sir Llewellyn, *Great Britain and the War of 1914-18* (London: Methuen & Co., 1967).

Reference works

Dictionnaire des Communes Administratif et Militaire France et

Departements Français D'Outre-Mer (Paris: Charles Lavau-
zelle & Cie, 1964).

*The Foreign Office List and Diplomatic and Consular Year Book
for 1914* (London: Harrison & Sons, 1914).

Hof- und Staats- Handbuch der Oesterreichisch—*Ungarischen Monarchie. Jahrgänge XLI, XLII, XLIII nach amtlichen Quellen
zusammengestellt* (Vienna: Druck und Verlag der K. K. Hof-
und Staatsdruckerei, 1915–1917).

*Militär Handbuch des Königreich Bayern herausgegeben für Per-
sönliche Angelegenheiten nach dem Stande von 16. Mai 1914,*
47. Auflage (Munich: Drucksachenverlag des Kriegsministe-
riums, 1914).

Foreword

It is not easy to understand the past. A good textbook helps by providing what its author—usually a distinguished historian—considers the essential facts and his interpretation of those facts. A good instructor also helps. But the student, if he is to be other than a parrot, must be exposed to more than one or two viewpoints. Told that authorities disagree, the student is likely to ask: "But which interpretation is *right?*"

At that point he is ready to do some research himself—to read and to evaluate what certain persons who actually saw an event wrote about it. Sampling original sources on which historical interpretations are based is not only an exciting experience; it adds flavor to knowledge. Furthermore, it encourages the student to weigh conflicting evidence himself and to understand historical variety and complexity.

The Primary Sources in American History series provides the documents necessary to explore the past through the eyes of those who lived it. Edited and introduced by an able scholar, each volume in the series contains contemporary material on some historical topic or period—either a collection of varied sources (letters, diaries, memoirs, reports, etc.), or a new edition of a classic eyewitness account.

Grady McWhiney
Editor

Preface

The documents for this book have been collected from the Public Record Office in London, the Haus-, Hof- und Staatsarchiv and the Kriegsarchiv in Vienna, the Bayrischen Hauptstaatsarchiv Abt. IV Kriegsarchiv, Munich, as well as the Hauptstaatsarchiv and Heeresarchiv in Stuttgart. Facsimiles of Crown copyright records in the Public Record Office appear by permission of the Controller of H. M. Stationery Office. The excerpt from "Sincere Desire for Peace. Submarine Warfare and America" by Hans Delbrück was taken and translated from *Krieg und Politik,* Volume III, with the permission of the Georg Stilke Verlag, Inc., Hamburg, Germany. I wish to thank both the representatives of the Verlag and of Professor Delbrück's heirs for their courtesy to me.

The archivists of the various archives which I have visited have been most helpful. I am in particular grateful to Oberregierungs-archivrat Dr. Jaeger, of the Bayrischen Hauptstaatsarchiv Abt. IV, Kriegsarchiv, and both Dr. Tadday of the Heeresarchiv and Dr. Bernd Ottnad of the Hauptstaatsarchiv in Stuttgart. My special gratitude is reserved for Dr. K. Peball of the Kriegsarchiv in Vienna, whose advice proved invaluable and in fact brought me to both Munich and Stuttgart. It was a pleasure to talk with him about history and to listen as he explained to me and other visitors what was available in his section of the Kriegsarchiv and how it could be best put to use. Finally let me thank Herr Spang of the

Heeresarchiv, Stuttgart, for all he told me about what was in the archives and for what he thought a military historian should think about when he tackles the problem of events now long past.

Forms of Address and Abbreviations

In every case full forms of address have been used in the first documents which have been translated. Where the same forms occur again and again, they have been abbreviated.

In the case of the Bavarian documents all reports, which are referred to by their M. Kr. file numbers in the Kriegsarchiv, were addressed to the Bavarian War Minister, who was rarely mentioned by name. The War Minister was Lieutenant General of the Cavalry Philipp von Hellingrath. The same is true of the reports to the Württemberg War Minister, Freiherr Carl von Weizäcker, who was also Minister of External Affairs.

The reports from German Supreme Headquarters to the Württemberg Minister of War are in the Heeresarchiv at Stuttgart in the file: *Persönliche Angelegenheiten des Württembergischen Kriegsministers. Berichte des Militärbevollmächtigten beim grossen Hauptquartier und des Stellvertretenden Militärbevollmächtigten in Berlin.* These reports are listed by volume as well as by month. Rather than using this full reference, the phrase *Persönliche Angelegenheiten des Württembergischen Kriegsministers* has been used, with the volume numbers. Where volumes referring to other series of the War Minister's files have been used, this has been noted.

British War Office and Foreign Office designations have been employed as they appeared on the documents.

The abbreviation GHQSM refers to the Supreme Headquarters of His Majesty, the Emperor, i.e., SM; it can also be rendered His Majesty's General Headquarters.

Dates are given in the European way, i.e., day, month, year; for example 2 January, 1918.

Robert C. Walton

Introduction

§ Anyone who reads this book hoping to learn more about the American doughboy and his adventures as an innocent abroad in the years between 1917 and 1919 will be disappointed. This book has been compiled as an attempt to allow Americans to see themselves as they were seen by Europeans (including the English, who at that time would not have permitted themselves to be classified with anyone else) during the years 1914 to 1918, especially 1917 to 1918.

The main emphasis has been placed upon the opinions of representatives of the Central Powers, Austria and Germany. References to English views have been made to provide contrast with the Central European attitudes. The French have been neglected. What is surprising is that the English and Austro-German opinions of and assumptions about the Americans were frequently very similar, though the English were far more elegant and effective in their dealings with them. The author believes that the book provides yet another confirmation of the truism so forcefully expressed by Robert Burns, that we never see ourselves as others see us.

The years 1914 to 1918 marked a turning point for the European powers, which until then had controlled the world. Even before the American intervention in April 1917, it was obvious that things would never be the same again, but no one could then perceive how rapidly and drastically they were going to change. One of the shrewder German observers, Hans Delbrück, was at least farsighted enough to see, as early as 1915, that the strain of the war would eventually cost Britain her empire. It took him longer to become aware of what price his own country would pay, but he began to realize it sooner than most. Before the war, the Polish-Jewish industrialist Ivor Bloch had recognized what a war fought by modern industrial states, using up-to-date weapons, would mean, and his books on the subject had thoroughly frightened the tsar of Russia. However, few statesmen and, as far as anyone can tell, far fewer soldiers paid any attention to Bloch.

The strain which the war imposed upon the resources of all the belligerents was enormous. It was remarkable that for at least the first two years of the war even the weakest of the contenders seemed to be able somehow to maintain their war effort. By 1917 this was no longer the case; revolution put Russia out of the war, and exhaustion, declining morale, and the unresolved aspirations of the subject nationalities turned Austria-Hungary into a liability for Germany. In the late spring of 1917, over fifty divisions of the French Army mutinied. If the Germans had known what was happening, they might well have exploited the situation and knocked France out of the war. But fate was kind to the French, and Pétain gained the time he needed to restore the confidence of the *poilu* in his commanders.

During 1917 and 1918 the main burden of confronting Germany in the West fell upon the English. The Commander in Chief of the British Expeditionary Force Field Marshal Douglas Haig and his advisers did not inform their own government exactly how serious the situation in the French Army was but claimed later that the British Army had to attack in Flanders in order to keep the Germans off balance, so that they would leave the French alone. They had little use for the latest French plan, which called for the Allies to remain on the defensive until the Americans arrived in sufficient numbers to make possible an attack upon the Germans with overwhelming superiority. Haig appears to have believed that his soldiers could defeat the Germans before the year was out and long before the addition of American forces could have a decisive effect. It is most probable that his desire for a British victory without significant American or French aid was the deciding factor in the decisions which led to the ill-fated and prolonged Passchendaele offensive.

The debate over the casualties suffered at Passchendaele still continues; at the time, they were enough to convince British Prime Minister David Lloyd George that Haig must not be allowed to launch any more such attacks. The Prime Minister was not politically strong enough to dismiss his top military commander, whom he did not trust, but he was able to deprive Haig of the extra troops he requested in order both to replenish the divisions weakened by participation in the campaign and to resume the attacks upon the German line in the spring of 1918. Lloyd George's mistrust of Haig was not the only reason for his decision to limit the number of replacements and reinforcements sent to France. England was in fact running dangerously short of manpower. Regardless of how justified Lloyd George may have been in cutting down the supply of soldiers to Haig's armies, the result was unfortunate.

The strategic initiative passed to the Germans. Their Western armies were reinforced by troops released from the Eastern Front as a result of Russia's collapse and, under the direction of First Quartermaster-General Erich Ludendorff, new tactics for breaching the enemy line were developed for the artillery and infantry. The best German troops were now organized in special units *(Sturmtruppen)* trained to exploit a breakthrough. Ludendorff was convinced that with two, or, if necessary, three attacks he could smash the British, cut them off from both their French allies and the channel ports and thus bring the war to an end by defeating the enemy in the field before the balance was tipped in favor of the Allies with the arrival of large numbers of American troops. Ludendorff came close to succeeding, but his plans lacked strategic coherence and his armies simply did not have the reserves to exploit fully the remarkable gains they made.

When the German assault came, the only source of fresh troops left to the Allies was the United States. It is sometimes forgotten that in late March 1918, when Ludendorff's *Sturmtruppen* emerged from the early morning mists to smash through the lines of Sir Hubert Gough's Fifth Army, the Allied High Command panicked. For the first time they agreed to coordinate their efforts more closely by accepting French Marshal Ferdinand Foch as the generalissimo of all Allied forces. Until March 21–22, 1918, no one on the Entente side had thought that it would be possible to use the Americans in large numbers before the summer of 1919. Sufficient shipping space and equipment were lacking for so many men, and above all the training of officers and troops for modern war was sadly lacking. Shortly after the first German attacks, Allied representatives in Washington were explaining to President Wilson and his Cabinet that the war would be lost if all the American infantry and machine gunners, even those who were only partially trained, were not sent to France immediately. The Americans met the request of their allies with remarkable alacrity. Much to everyone's surprise, the British located the shipping, and the Americans provided hundreds of thousands of troops each month for what became the last great effort to stop and defeat the Germans. It was perhaps the final irony for the Germans that the very extent of their success in the spring of 1918 brought about the arrival of American troops well before either side had expected them.

The presence of the Americans was decisive, and the Entente, though almost as exhausted as the Central Powers, won the war. However, American aid was not obtained without difficulty. Long before the spring crisis the Allies had asked that American units be attached to French and British divisions. General John Joseph Pershing, the commander of the American Expeditionary Force, had objected to such a

procedure but had finally agreed to allow certain American
formations to serve with Allied divisions for training purposes. During the spring of 1918 President Wilson had supported fully the Allied request that American machine gunners and infantrymen be used to make good the losses
suffered by British and French divisions. Wilson's willingness
to do this meant that the troops sent were not balanced units
capable of being expanded quickly into divisional formations.
General Pershing was strongly opposed to employing American troops in this way. It appears that he never quite realized
how serious the situation was on the Western Front and
suspected that the reports he was receiving were deliberately
given a pessimistic cast, so that he would relinquish command
of troops which were rightfully his. He was determined that
American troops should fight in an American field army under an American commander, and he was a very stubborn
man. Pershing drove the British and French to despair. They
felt that they had some reason for believing that he was really
an ally of Ludendorff.

The Allies needed American support too badly to deny
Pershing's wishes for any length of time. Indeed well into
September, three months after the tide had in fact turned,
Haig and the Chief of the Imperial General Staff, Sir Henry
Wilson, feared that their own armies could not stand another
winter's campaign and that a negotiated peace would be necessary unless Germany could be defeated before the start of
winter. Troops brigaded with English and French formations
were gradually returned to American command, and by June
American divisions made their first independent attacks,
though in this instance with plenty of French guidance. Three
months later, in September, an American Army assailed the
German salient along the Marne. The cost to the Americans
was a large number of unnecessary casualties, which was the
natural result of their inexperience at all levels of command,
but an American Army fought under its own leaders in
France.

The psychological effect of the appearance of large num-

bers of American troops who were neither tired of war nor
lacking in anything but the skill at arms of veteran soldiers,
which they would learn soon enough, on top of the failure of
the great spring offensive proved too much for the German
soldiers at the front. Their morale began to crack. Although
there were increasing difficulties among soldiers on garrison
duty at home and unrest among the civilian population was
becoming a problem for the German government, the German Army was not stabbed in the back by the home front.
After four years of grueling struggle, it faced a foe which was
being reinforced by a seemingly endless flow of men and
material. The German military leadership, which had in fact
governed the Empire since 1916, had failed to assess accurately the capability of the United States (with the aid of its
allies, who had to provide much of the equipment) to put an
army of well over 2,000,000 men in the field within the space
of a year and a half. It was the knowledge that the Imperial
Army was beaten on the field of battle which on the 28th of
September 1918 caused Ludendorff to roll on the floor, foam
at the mouth and then, when he had somewhat recovered
control of himself, to demand an immediate armistice. Ludendorff's sudden desire for an armistice was in part responsible
for the situation that resulted. The diplomats of the Foreign
Office sued for peace; even as they did, revolution swept
away the government they served. The war did not end with a
negotiated peace, for the Americans had brought victory in
the field to the Allies. America's friends were almost as
surprised as her enemies, but far more pleasantly.

Of course President Wilson soon discovered that it would
not be possible to make the defeated powers, let alone all of
Europe, a school of democracy. The great majority of the
Americans who had been "over there" voted against Wilson
and his policies almost as soon as they returned home and
were able to leave the armed forces. They desired something
both for themselves and for their country which seemed to
them far more important than further foreign adventures.

Warren Gamaliel Harding summed up what they wanted: "A return to normalcy"!

Europe never quite got the chance to return to "normalcy." The Germans brooded over their defeat, the Versailles Treaty, and the Weimar Republic. For many Germans the best explanation was that the Imperial Army had been stabbed in the back by the home front, which had been subverted by the communists and socialists. The Allied nations also brooded in their way. The damage done by the war was not so immediately apparent, but it was there. The French hoped that the limitation of the German Army to 100,000 men, reparations payments, and a system of alliance with the East European succession states would make good their losses and at least partially insure them against a future German threat. The British had their empire, and indeed it had become larger. They were still a rich industrial nation, or so it seemed, and they believed that they had fought a long war for a just and righteous cause.

What they resented more than the French was the troublesome American claim that the United States had saved the Allies just in the nick of time. Uncouth tourists, noisy veterans' organizations, and loquacious American politicians never ceased to mention this. It seemed both unfair and untrue, for what did the Americans know of the years of sacrifice and those terrible casualty lists, or the pictures published weekly in the *London Illustrated News* of the young officers who had fallen? After all, the Germans never quite got through the Fifth Army, nor had they reached Amiens. These had been British and French, not American, shows. It seemed to many that about all the Americans had done was to get rich from the sufferings of others, and indeed the United States was now a creditor nation. Her political leaders had a habit of mentioning this claim too. All of this was so unpleasant and quite wrong.

What everyone was glad to forget was the frightening strength of manpower resources and industrial potential, as well as organizational skill, which the United States had revealed only briefly during the closing phase of the war. Though many had seen the advantages the United States had to offer as an ally before she entered the conflict, no one had believed that she would be able to bring her assets to bear so rapidly and so effectively. The Allies had miscalculated as badly as the Germans. The result was that Europe was changed beyond recognition by that intervention, and no one quite understood what had happened. Perhaps after the war everyone should have been glad that the Americans had decided to return to what they considered "normalcy." How far the Americans were able to tip the balance of power on the Continent should have been a warning and an inducement for closer cooperation between the nations of Europe to prevent the trauma of large-scale American military and diplomatic tourism from recurring. Despite the League of Nations, no such cooperation really took place. This was the case at least in part because it would have meant dealing with Bolshevik Russia, a most unpleasant and undesirable by-product of the war. It was left to the defeated and disgraced Germans to do that.

Major General John Frederick Fuller was probably wrong when he said that American intervention prevented a negotiated settlement. The military and, to a surprising extent, the civilian authorities on both sides wanted a victory and because they did, the Americans became involved.

The first portion of this book attempts to shed some light upon how the Americans did become involved. It has been argued that America had a real interest in preventing Germany from upsetting the balance of power in Europe and that her entry into the war followed logically from the need to protect American interests. The selection of documents presented here reveals that the representatives of the Central Powers were never quite sure what the American interests were. It is also at least fair to add that the American government did not always seem to be entirely sure, either. American policy after the war indicates that there was no lasting general consensus in the United States about American aims and policy in Europe.

The failure of the diplomats who represented the Central Powers to understand America's aims was in part due to arrogance and a real inability to understand either the dynamics of American democracy or the moral tone in which American policy statements were delivered. They insisted on believing that the United States was also playing the game of realistic power politics as they conceived of it. At best they were only half right. This inability to assess with real accuracy the factors which motivated American behavior was common to the governments and ruling classes of the Central European monarchies. To be sure this blind spot was not merely confined to their relations with America. It is significant that for all the good intentions of Theobald von Bethmann Hollweg, the Imperial Chancellor, he and Germany's other civilian leaders had accepted the Schlieffen plan as the final solution to the problem of Germany's diplomatic isolation. Once the plan failed, Germany's leaders did not really seem to understand what kind of a war this failure had produced.

It is significant that the representatives of the Central Powers, as well as those of the Entente, agreed completely on one point: America's importance as a Pacific power. When the United States armed for war, it was widely assumed that she was also preparing for a conflict with Japan for the domination of the Pacific. The British were almost as emphatic about this as the Austrians and Germans. At least some of their diplomatic observers assumed that a war with Japan which would involve both the United States and the United Kingdom was more than likely.

However, the general difficulty which the Central Powers and their representatives found in developing a viable policy towards America left a vacuum which the soldiers, who had come to dominate the policy of the German government, filled with the claim that victory could only be achieved through unrestricted submarine warfare. The naval experts had endless statistics which proved that the submarine was the ultimate weapon with which England could be defeated. They insisted that it was worth the risk of an American declaration of war because England would be out of the war before the Americans could possibly make any direct military contribution, except to participate in the peace negotiations with a victorious German empire. Bethmann Hollweg gave up the struggle against the military probably because in the end they seemed more formidable to him than did America under Woodrow Wilson. After all, it must be recognized that Bethmann had to deal with Ludendorff, which was an unenviable task under the best of circumstances. Despite Ludendorff, the Austrian Chief of Staff, Field Marshal Francis Count Conrad von Hötzendorf, continued to press his doubts. He wrote a discreet letter to the *Grossen Hauptquartier* in which he stated his case, but his dismissal had already been arranged before the letter was posted.

Germany's hope for victory now rested upon a piece of fragile, complicated naval gadgetry, the submarine, and long lists of statistics, recording the tonnage of Allied ships sunk each month. Military expedients in the form of new weapons and tactics had taken the place of a sound, coordinated foreign policy. The result was the kind of hopeless military situation involving incredibly heavy losses which the final portion of this book describes.

The British and French leaders were more realistic about the Americans. The Allies had already profited greatly from the financial aid organized for them in the United States under the direction of the House of Morgan. They were also better able to draw upon the raw materials and manufactured goods American industry was glad to sell to them, because the British Navy had driven the German merchant fleet from the sea soon after the war began. Though the British ambassador, Sir Cecil Spring-Rice, did not always think so, Paris and London were quite sure that Woodrow Wilson really sympathized more with them than he did with the Germans. Their representatives knew far better than the k.u.k. ambassador Constantine Dumba or Count Bernsdorff how to appeal to his Calvinist sense of righteousness. They saw American entry into the war as the final guarantee of an Allied victory, and their respective foreign offices exercised great patience and tact to overcome the pressure which operated against American entry into the struggle. In the end, despite even William Jennings Bryan, they succeeded. However neither the diplomatic nor the military representatives of the Allies believed that the United States would be able to play a major military role in the war. American help was conceived of as financial and industrial, and not primarily military. A close look at the size, training, and armament of the U.S. Army in 1917 explains why. The U.S. Navy was far more important.

Documents for this book were collected from the Public Record office in London, the Haus-, Hof- und Staatsarchiv and the Kriegsarchiv in Vienna, the Bayrischen Hauptstaatsarchiv Abt. IV Kriegsarchiv, Munich, as well as the Hauptstaatsarchiv and Heeresarchiv in Stuttgart.

The Bavarian and Württemberg Archives contain the daily reports from the chiefs of the military missions of these federal states at German Supreme Headquarters to their respective Ministers of War. Among the Bavarian reports are a number of special policy papers which discuss very frankly the declining chances of a German victory after June 1918. These reports, as well as excerpts taken from the War Diaries of the XIII Army Corps and the group of armies which were under the command of Duke Albert of Württemberg, give a graphic description of the impact of the American forces upon the German troops in the field. The papers from Vienna contain the reports of the Austrian representatives in Washington and the conclusions of the Imperial and Royal Intelligence Service. When read in conjunction with some of the German diplomatic material, they are of great interest.

The material drawn from these collections is at best only a

selection of what is there. It slights the vast collection of German Diplomatic and other government documents which were microfilmed in the United States after World War II and subsequently returned to the German Government. However the selection as it stands is intended to serve the needs of students of American History and to stimulate the undergraduate to go on and look for himself. It also seeks to attract a wider audience drawn from many other walks of life.

Detroit   August 1971

CHAPTER I

The Last Months of Peace

§ The reports contained in this section date from the last months of peace in Europe. The British view of the American scene was more detached but quite similar in almost every respect to that expressed by the k.u.k. naval attaché, Korvetten-Kapitän (Lieutenant Commander) Maximilian Burstyn,[1] in late 1913 and early 1914.

According to the British ambassador, Sir Cecil Spring-Rice, war with Mexico was the main concern of the American government and the newspapers. As Sir Cecil saw the matter, domestic politics would ultimately determine the future course of American relations with Mexico, as they already had in the case of Cuba. He believed that for the moment the Mexican affair was diverting attention from the "movement towards social reform which has left such a deep

---

[1] Burstyn returned to Austria shortly after war was declared and was killed in action in the Gulf of Cattaro in 1917. The *Hof- und Staats-Handbuch* continued to list Burstyn as the naval attaché until the end of 1917. *Hof- und Staats-Handbuch der Oesterreichisch-Ungarischen Monarchie. Nach amtlichen Quellen zusammengestellt,* Jahrgänge XLI-XLIII (1915–1917) (Wien: Druck und Verlag der K.K. Hof-und Staatsdruckerei 1915–1917). This in itself reveals a good deal about the machinery of the imperial bureaucracy during the last years of the Monarchy. The failure to appoint an attaché deprived Vienna of any reliable firsthand reports of American military potential during this crucial period. I have taken Burstyn's reports from the records of the *Präsidial Kanzlei* – XII 9/1.

mark on the history of politics here during the past few years."[2] In connection with this movement Spring-Rice noted the changing attitude of the American public towards the role of the federal government in the realm of social reform.

The concluding section of Spring-Rice's report dealt with the efforts of Secretary of the Navy Josephus Daniels to introduce democracy and prohibition into the Navy. Daniels, who was a Southerner, gave up his attempt to compel officers and men to mess together when he was informed that this would require whites to eat with blacks. Though the Ambassador had little confidence in Daniels, he was fair enough to put his order prohibiting the use of alcohol into a larger context. Similar efforts were being made by the Canadian Minister of Defence, and in the past the Duke of Wellington himself had undertaken to prohibit smoking in the British Army. Sir Cecil believed that even Woodrow Wilson showed a tendency toward the same kind of "ineptitude" which had made Secretary Daniels a figure of fun, but he concluded that Daniels's activities probably served the interests of the Democratic Party in the Midwest.[3]

The three reports of Korvetten-Kapitän Maximilian Burstyn reprinted below discuss the significance of Wilson's and Secretary Daniels's attitudes towards the American armed services. They do not show the same perspective revealed in Sir Cecil Spring-Rice's memorandum, but they tell us a lot about how a European viewed the American scene some fifty years ago. Burstyn's report on the entry of immigrants from the Dual Monarchy into the American armed services is particularly interesting both for the light it sheds on the plight of the immigrant in America and the attitude of the emigrant's home country. The reader should remember that a citizen of Austria-Hungary who joined the American Army was automatically a deserter from the k.u.k. Army, and in pre-1914 Europe desertion was a very serious matter.

[2] F.O. 371/2153/7893
[3] Ibid.

F.O. 371/2153/7893. North America. Confidential.

Confidential

Sir C. Spring-Rice to Sir Edmund Grey (Received May 22)

No. 153.   WASHINGTON, May 11, 1914

SIR,

Since Easter, when my last fortnightly report was written, events have taken a turn which makes any reasoned study of internal politics very difficult. It is probably true that the country at large still cares very little about Mexico, and knows less; but Washington, at the moment of writing, feels that the nation lies already under the shadow of war, and it is hard for those who know the danger of the situation — and for the press which profits by its sensational features — to devote attention to any other subject.

It must, however, be remembered that even those whose thoughts are dominated by the approach of the storm are inclined, if they have ever expended any thought on internal politics, to judge the situation in Mexico in terms of the domestic situation in the United States. Such men are troubled by the doubt how far the country will be able to work out the solution of its constitutional problems, or continue the movement towards social reform which has left such a deep mark on the history of politics here during the past few years, if its attention is now diverted to such far-reaching responsibilities abroad as intervention in Mexico would inevitably entail. And consequently, should intervention be undertaken, its nature, its duration, and its outcome will probably depend less upon the needs of Mexico than upon the trend of internal politics. It has often been whispered that the last evacuation of Cuba by the United States, coinciding as it did closely with the end of Colonel Roosevelt's administration, was premature, and effected without due regard to the interests of the island and with undue regard to party exigencies in the United States. This history may well repeat itself, and the tendencies of internal politics here may therefore be said to gain an added significance, however much those tendencies may seemed obscured by external preoccupations.

In domestic affairs the most striking event is, without question, the "labour war" in the Colorado mines. The economic and industrial questions at issue in this strike belong to the commercial reports. Here it may be sufficient to draw attention to one remarkable feature, namely, the manner in which the intervention of the Federal troops has been received. The Federal Government sent troops at the request of the Governor of Colorado after the State militia had, if accounts are true, shown both inefficiency and brutality. The feeling in the State toward the arrival of the troops is thus summarised by one review: "The coming of the United States troops seems to have been welcomed by the strike leaders, the operators, and the distracted State, county, and local officials. It is no less welcome to the newspapers of the country. . . . . The troops . . . ., as certain editors point out, will handle the situation as neutrals, whereas the State militia have been freely accused of siding with the operators." The curious thing in this is the gradual change it marks. Twenty years ago, in the Chicago Pullman strike, President Cleveland sent Federal troops in the face of the strongest remonstrance from Governor Altgeld, of Illinois, and it may be safely said that radical opinion supported the Governor. Some years later President Roosevelt sent troops into Nevada, but this time at the Governor's request, and it was the President who, according to his own account, desired to withdraw the troops as soon as possible in order to force the reluctant State to live up to its responsibilities. Since that time in Pennsylvania, and within the last year in West Virginia, the drastic action of the State troops has been bitterly criticised by the labour unions and by all sections of radical opinion, and, though the cases above quoted were not identical in their circumstances, the present strike is an indication of the growing popular confidence in the Federal as compared with the State Governments, and of the decay of "States rights" feeling among the people at large. If the history of the "Federal experiment" in America has any lesson to teach, it is that, while in the early days of a federation the separate States may represent themselves as fighting for liberty against the Federal power, yet as the nation develops and new conceptions of liberty and government are evolved these conceptions tend to be confided to the care of the Central Government, and the allegiance of radical opinion to be transferred to it.

The tendency of radical opinion to turn its eyes to the Federal Government has indeed awkward results for Congress. Two proposals are now before that body which Congressmen have long desired to shirk—the question of woman suffrage and the question of national prohibition. Both these proposals have for their object the super-session of State action by an amendment to the Federal Con-stitution, and both have sufficient support in the country to make Congressmen very reluctant to vote against them.

The State Governments are themselves conscious of this tenden-cy, and their tone in dealing with such questions is gradually chang-ing. The Western Conference of Governors which has just been meeting at Denver has passed a resolution regarding conservation which rings very differently from former defences of State rights in this same matter. "It is the duty of every State," says this resolution, "to adopt such laws as will make for true conservation of our resources, prevent monopoly, and render the greatest good to the greatest number; and as rapidly as the States prepare themselves to carry out such a policy the Federal Government should withdraw its supervision and turn the work over to the States." What was pre-viously regarded as the right of the States thus seems to be now represented by the States themselves as a concession to good behav-iour.

A recent election in Illinois has given women their first opportu-nity in that State to show the effect of the newly-won suffrage. The result appears to have shown a very marked tendency towards the introduction of prohibition in the counties, as has been the case elsewhere, but except on the liquor question the woman's vote does not appear to have been "solid," or to have produced any distinct effect.

Recent municipal elections have resulted in another defeat for the Socialists at Milwaukee, but on the other hand the Socialist candi-dates have been successful at Jamestown, New York, and Missoula, Montana.

As an indication of popular social reform feeling it may be worth while to enumerate the proposals of the Indiana State Progressive platform, viz., national prohibition (endorsed also by the Progres-sives of Ohio and Maine), abolition of injunctions in labour disputes, laws compelling ample notice before a strike or lockout, minimum wage for women, initiative, referendum, and recall, primary law, short ballot, woman suffrage, and home rule for cities. The Mexican and Colombian policies of the Administration come in, as usual, for severe criticism.

From such high matters it seems hard to come down to the

immediate questions of party politics, but one recent occurrence has once more drawn attention to the fact that the chief weakness of the Administration is the difficulty of taking some of its members seriously. Next to Mr. Bryan, who after all has exposed himself only to sectional ridicule, for the Middle West is still inclined to admire qualities at which New York laughs, and who still exerts great influence with many Congressmen on internal questions, the Cabinet officer who inspires least confidence is the Secretary of the Navy. He starts with the initial disabilities of a Christian name which is a godsend to humorists and a face in which self-satisfaction, muddleheadedness, and the milk of human kindness struggle for the mastery over expression. But, unfortunately, he has shown a tendency to live up to these accidental and natural defects. His first *faux pas* last year was to attempt to issue an order to the effect that officers and men should in future mess together; he refrained, however, from this action when it was pointed out that he, a southerner, would thereby be forcing white gentlemen to dip their hand in the same dish with Negroes. He has now issued an order prohibiting the use of any alcoholic beverage in the navy, and this action has been greeted with storms of criticism and ridicule. It is all very well, however, to represent him as an old woman exercising grandmotherly supervision over the morals of the navy, but it is not easy to see wherein his action differs from, for instance, the Duke of Wellington's general order against smoking, or the wish recently expressed informally by the Canadian Minister of Defence that no liquor should be used in militia messes. What his action really shows is not foolishness of policy so much as ineptitude of method; any needed reform could have been accomplished quietly without official instructions published broadcast and justified by the Secretary by an appeal to his own private teetotal conscience. It is this ineptitude, from which, unfortunately, the President himself is not wholly free, which threatens the life of the Administration, at any rate in the sophisticated East, though it is probable that a large element of simple-minded opinion in the West is still sufficiently hostile to the "idle militarists" of the army and navy to greet any "tail-twisting" administered to those services with a certain smug approval.

I have, &c.

CECIL SPRING-RICE

§   A dinner meeting of the Carabao Club, made up of officers of the armed forces who had served in the Philippines, aroused the wrath of President Wilson. During the course of the dinner the government, its leaders, and its policies had been the subject of critical satire. This was no laughing matter for Woodrow Wilson, but Lieutenant Commander Burstyn saw things from a different point of view.

K.u.k. Naval Attaché, Washington, to
the k.u.k War Ministry, Naval Section, Vienna

Behavior of officers on the occasion of the Carabao Dinner.

No. 140

WASHINGTON, 23 December, 1913

The Carabao Club is made up of officers of both the Army and the Navy who have been stationed in the Philippines.

On the occasion of the yearly banquet held in Washington during December, speeches have been and are made which contain more or less sharp criticism of the government, its principal officials, and of conditions in the Philippine Islands.

It is understandable that in the United States the generally accepted belief in the right to personal freedom of expression in the spoken and written word often allows one to go very far indeed.

The speeches made at this year's dinner and especially the song "Damn the Insurrectos" have aroused the displeasure of the President and members of the Cabinet, and Mr. Wilson has ordered a careful investigation.

I do not understand why objections have been made this year to a song, which dates from 1899 and was sung every year under the Republican administration.

As can be seen from the enclosed clippings, President Wilson has ordered that all the participants in the dinner receive a severe reprimand for their conduct.

In military circles there is great astonishment and dismay over the proceedings of the Democratic regime.

Up till now the Democrats have done nothing to raise the esteem of officers. Indeed they have rather damaged the officers' own conception of their place in society.

If the rumor which is circulating here is true, then it is not surprising that officers are embittered against the representatives of their government. It is reported that, while making a speech at an army camp in Texas, Secretary of State Bryan took occasion to tell the men that he could not understand why they did not prefer a respectable civilian profession to that of service in the Army.

The officer corps of the United States is in such a difficult position that I am always amazed there are still people to be found who enter the Army or Navy. Such service gives them no social standing. Getting along with the men was already an art and now, when the Democrats are using every means to introduce the principle of equality into the military, it will soon become an impossibility.

Navy Secretary Daniels is said to have shaken the hands of two stokers on a visit to a battleship. When he noticed that the Admiral who accompanied him did not follow his example, he is reported to have asked: "Do you think that you are too good to shake the hand of a sailor?"

It is certainly an advantage for the United States and for the maintenance of discipline in the Army and Navy if there are limits to freedom in what one may say and write. It is also necessary for public officials to try to strengthen the authority of the officers and not to undermine further the position of officers with their men.

BURSTYN KK.

1 Enclosure

§   The article reads as follows:

HARD ON THE CARABAO

Dinner Committee Must Read
Wilson's Stinging Letter,
Thus to be Reprimanded

Copies, Under Order of Secretaries Garrison and Daniels, Will Be Sent to Officers Who Are Responsible for Program Given Recently, in Which Cabinet Officers Were "Ridiculed."

President Wilson yesterday made public a letter addressed to Secretaries Garrison and Daniels, respectively, requesting that a "very serious reprimand" be administered to those army and navy officers who participated in the recent dinner of the Military Order of the Carabao, at which the administration's Philippine and other policies were satirized. The letter follows:

"The officers who were responsible for the program of the evening are certainly deserving of a very serious reprimand, which I hereby request be administered, and I cannot rid myself of a feeling of great disappointment that the general body of officers assembled at the dinner should have greeted the carrying out of such a program with apparent indifference to the fact that it violated one of the most dignified and sacred traditions of the service.

Assails Their Idea of "Fun."

"I am told that the songs and other amusements of the evening were intended and regarded as 'fun.' What are we to think of officers of the army and navy of the United States who think it 'fun' to bring their official superiors into ridicule and the policies of the government which they are sworn to serve with unquestioning loyalty into contempt? If this is their idea of fun, what is their ideal of duty? If they do not hold their loyalty above all silly effervescences of childish wit, what about their profession do they hold sacred?

Recalls Them to Their Ideals

"My purpose, therefore, in administering this reprimand is to recall the men who are responsible for this lowering of standards to their ideals; to remind them of the high conscience with which they ought to put duty above personal indulgence, and to think of themselves as responsible men and trusted soldiers, even while they are amusing themselves as diners out. Sincerely yours,

"WOODROW WILSON"

Will Get Copies of the Letter.

Secretaries Garrison and Daniels decided to administer the reprimand by transmitting a copy of the President's letter to each member of the entertainment committee.

Secretary Garrison immediately sent this memorandum to
Maj. Gen. Leonard Wood, chief of staff of the army:

"It is hereby ordered that the officers of the United
States army who were on the dinner committee, and
were therefore responsible for the program of entertainment at the recent dinner of the Military Order of the
Carabao, held December 11, 1913, be reprimanded in
pursuance of the communication of the President to me
dated December 22, 1913, copy herewith. The form that
the reprimand should take should be to furnish to each
of said officers a copy of the letter from the President."

Secretary Daniels probably will issue a similar order today,
making the presidential rebuke effective as far as navy officers
are concerned.

DAMN, DAMN, DAMN THE INSURRECTOS

In that land of dopy dreams, happy, peaceful Philippines,
　　Where the boloman is hiking night and day,
Where Tagalos steal and lie, where Americanos die,
　　There you hear the soldiers sing this evening lay:

Chorus

Damn, damn, damn the insurrectos, cross-eyed kakiack lad-
　　rones,
　　Underneath the starry flag, civilize 'em with a Krag.
And return us to our own beloved homes.

There's a land of dopy dreams, far from Filipino themes,
　　Where the bolomen are busy night and day;
Where they wield the gladsome ax, taking huge and gory
　　hacks,
　　At a shining pate or lock or hoary hair.

Old time customs there are few, all the members hack and hew
　　At the standpat bunch in manner far from nice.
They believe in making Hay, Warren for it day by day,
　　When the pie is cut each wants the biggest slice.

I've a large and growing hunch that this insurrecto bunch
　　Would have been the chaps to cop the fleece of gold;

Poor old Jason in his hunt would have pulled a better stunt,
    Had he the crowd that left us in the cold.

§   A subsequent report was filled with sympathy for the
American Navy officer. Burstyn told his superiors on April
9, 1914, that, as of the first of July, 1914, Secretary Daniels
had forbidden the possession and consumption of alcohol
upon the ships and in the shore bases of the United States
Navy. He noted one ray of hope for the Navy: Secretary
Daniels had allowed the new regulation to be waived for such
events as the fleet review scheduled for 1915.

Imperial and Royal Naval Attaché, Washington, to
the Imperial and Royal War Ministry,
Naval Section, Vienna

Prohibition of alcohol on Naval ships and in Naval stations.

No. 38   WASHINGTON, 9 April, 1914

There is profound and indeed well justified indignation in Navy
circles at this ridiculous tutelage and there is great fear of mockery
by foreign nations.
    It is natural that the American daily press and humor magazines
exploit this theme with the ruthlessness typical of the country, in
order to make fun of Daniels in cartoons and articles.
    Daniels, like most of his colleagues, is a teetotaler. If this regu-
lation was merely the result of his own personal belief, it might
perhaps be easier to come to terms with, rather than with the all too
well justified assumption that this order, like so many orders which
have been issued in the past, has a political motivation.
    This time the main reason for the regulation is that the pursuit of
popularity among the masses succeeds best with the slogan "the
same law for all" and therefore officers are not to be favored above
the men.
    What I cannot understand is that Daniels could take such a
decisive step without previously obtaining the approval of the President.

As far as is known to date the Secretary of War does not intend to issue a similar prohibition for army officers.

BURSTYN KK.

§   A letter which sounded a more somber note was dispatched by Burstyn on June 17, 1914. It dealt with the recruitment of newly arrived immigrants for the American Army. As the report reveals, the uninformed new arrival was sometimes sadly misled about his obligations to serve in the armed forces of his adopted country.

K.u.k. Naval Attaché, Washington, to
the k.u.k War Ministry Naval Section, Vienna

The enlistment of foreigners in the American Army.

No. 87   WASHINGTON, 17 June, 1914

As far as is possible all obstacles to the enlistment of foreigners in the American Army and Navy are removed.

American citizenship is not a requirement for enrollment, but rather it is sufficient if the recruit promises to apply for citizenship after two years.

If the applicant is not of age, he must have either his parents or someone authorized to do so state upon his application form that there is no objection to his early entry into the armed services.

I believe I am correct in saying that there are always people to be found who, though they have no right to do this, give their signature for this purpose in return for a fee. I found the signature of one "Simon Wolfhart" upon the application form of a young Austrian who was scarcely seventeen years old. A letter from the father to the k.u.k General Consulate in New York with the urgent request that all possible steps be taken to free his son from service indicates that the parents did not approve of his entry into the American Army.

In many cases it happens that young people are compelled by lack of employment and hunger to seek enlistment and thus become deserters. Most immigrants who come to the United States still believe that one can earn money here very easily. But this is not the case, especially in recent years.

Most of the industrial cities are overcrowded and it is in exactly these areas that the immigrants customarily settle. Laborers are needed here chiefly for farm labor but the majority of immigrants, who have emigrated primarily because they could find no work at home in the cities, do not want to work here on farms either.

Therefore it is all too easy to explain, why people who are without work and close to starvation would gladly allow themselves to be recruited to find a way out of their predicament. 50 cents (. . .) a day with free food and clothing and the prospect of a pension sounds attractive and therefore many a young man, who perhaps may have never intended to become a deserter, lets himself be recruited to become involuntarily an American citizen and thereby to be lost forever to his homeland.

When one considers that in the last 10 months about 225,000 people have emigrated from Austria and Hungary alone, there is a certain justification for asserting that not all of them found employment immediately and that consequently a certain percentage fell victim to the recruiting "business."

Among the American people there is no great predilection for entry into the Army or Navy in peacetime. Service is viewed here as a "business" and, as one often hears, as a bad "business." The uniform enjoys no particular respect which the signs "No man in uniform admitted," though legally forbidden, but still found on restaurants, prove.

It is known that it is difficult — and often impossible — for the American Army and Navy to fill their ranks.

Washington is not the proper place for the study of this, in my opinion, extremely important question, because immigrants very seldom appear here.

It is certainly not for me to make proposals in such a matter and I venture to do so only because I consider the question of immigration to be so important. As far as I know the officials in the k.u.k. consular offices are so overburdened that it is not possible to impose upon them any additional work. Therefore I believe that a remedy could be found by appointing officers to the consulates in New York, Pittsburgh, Chicago, etc.

But these officers should not only study the question of immigration, they should also take over the military responsibility for the memorandum-book, i.e., giving to the immigrants all the information about military matters which they desire, being present at enlistments of minors, aiding in finding employment, etc.

I believe that I am not mistaken when I assume that after one to two years of official activity all the desired information about the question of immigration which requires consideration from the military point of view can be gathered from the reports of these officers.

BURSTYN M.P., KORVETTEN-KAPITÄN

CHAPTER **II**

Europe at War and the Submarine, 1915–16

VIEWS OF AMERICA DURING THE EARLY STAGES OF THE WAR

§   All sides still had hopes of attracting American support, though the representatives of the Central Powers were rightly less optimistic. A long letter from a British representative, Lancelot Hugh Smith, to Sir Gilbert Parker, who directed the English propaganda campaign in the United States, bearing the dateline 23 Wall Street, New York, December 4, 1914, reveals how justified a certain pessimism on the part of the German and Austrian diplomats was. The second paragraph of the letter began:

I write from the office of J. P. Morgan & Co. where I have a private room, and they give out that I am here for their London firm. J. P. Morgan has been of the greatest service to me, both in giving me advice, asking people to meet me and telling me what he hears.

Morgan had assigned an aid to Mr. Smith with the assurance that he was "absolutely loyal to him and to England." As far

15

as the British representative was concerned things could not be better, and he was particularly pleased to inform Sir Gilbert about anti-German sentiment in New York: "I am astounded at the feeling for the Allies and the bitterness against the Germans." The President of the Federal Reserve Bank, "(the Govt Bk. which is to try and take the place of the Bank of England in New York)," Mr. Strong, had explained to Smith that anti-German feeling was the result of the reports about Belgian atrocities.

There were of course certain clouds on the horizon. One major banking house, Kuhn Loeb & Co., was pro-German, to which fact Smith hastened to add "but then they are Jews, and you will know the feeling about Jews here." The remainder of the letter dealt with contraband items and the need to coordinate Allied purchasing in the United States. The letter leaves little doubt where the sympathies of the financial community were.[1]

But New York was not America. G. M. Trevelyan's official report on his speaking tour of the East and Midwest, which was delivered in May 1915, revealed that there was strong pro-Allied feeling in both these regions. According to Trevelyan, there was even hope that a pro-Allied voting block would be organized among Slavic immigrants to counteract the German vote. The universities were also behind the Allies, and Trevelyan found a reaction against German intellectual domination underway among American academics which he hoped would serve to bring more American scholars to England after the war. However, he added that to profit from this development English universities would have to care "for our 'cousins' in a less parochial spirit than has sometimes formerly obtained." It was Trevelyan's impression that even the traditionally anti-British feeling of old-stock Americans had changed in part because "the Anglo-Saxon element in the United States is now a minority."

---

[1] F.O. 371/2226/XC 7791.

There were essentially two strands of feeling: (1) "Pro-English feeling" and (2) "Anti-German feeling." The *Lusitania* incident had stimulated the latter in particular and, as Trevelyan saw it, had counteracted resentment against British interference with American trade. He added that Lord Bryce's report on enemy atrocities that appeared the day after the *Lusitania* was sunk "received absolute credence" because of the sinking.[2] Despite these very positive factors, Trevelyan felt constrained to say that the majority of Americans did not want to be involved in the war.

The report closed with some comments on leading personalities of the day. Roosevelt "has no real weight at present" and Wilson "takes no *personal* advice, either from his colleagues, his relations, or his friends. He is a very lonely man in the White House, ..." Trevelyan assured his government that the British policy toward America was on the whole successful.[3]

A report of the British consul in New York, C. W. Bennett, to Lord Grey in December 1914 illustrates one element which complicated Anglo-American relations: the Irish question. The editor of the *Gaelic American,* John W. Devvy, had said that England's enemies were Ireland's friends and the syndicalist Jim Larkin was appealing to young Irishmen to return home to Ireland to fight for their country.[4] Trevelyan had also referred to this difficulty but he, like the Consul, did not believe that the majority of Irish-Americans were actually anti-Ally.

It is clear that a very crucial factor in molding public opinion in favor of the Entente was the sinking of the passenger liner *Lusitania,* which was one of a number of spectacular sinkings involving the loss of American lives. In view of the Tirpitz Naval Armaments program it is particularly ironic that the submarine was the only offensive weapon the Ger-

---

[2] The report was anything but accurate.
[3] F.O. 371/2558/7892.
[4] F.O. 371/2226/85776.

man Navy possessed which had a real potential for affecting the British war effort and could be employed in response to the ever-more effective British blockade of German trade. One major problem with the submarine was that it was very vulnerable; indeed its construction made it a fragile commerce raider as long as it followed the accepted rules of warfare—approached its prey on the surface, fired a shot across its bow, searched it for contraband if the ship flew a neutral flag, and, if not, gave the crew time to abandon ship before sinking the vessel. After this it was expected that the crew would be taken aboard the raider or that provision would be made for them to reach land or a neutral port. It was relatively easy to arm merchantmen, as the British did, to disguise fighting ships as merchant vessels, or even as neutrals, and sink the surfaced submarine with fire from deck guns. The "unrestricted" use of the submersible craft, which allowed the U-boat to approach (or more likely await its prey) unseen and sink it without warning, offered protection to the submarine against such armament, as well as real opportunities to disrupt enemy commerce. The Germans claimed they had to employ the submarine this way because the British armed their merchant vessels. The problem was that a submarine firing when submerged could not always avoid sinking neutrals or passenger ships, which, though classified as "noncombatant" vessels, might well be carrying troops and contraband, as well as civilians.

The Germans declared British waters to be a war zone in which "unrestricted" use of the submarine would be made early in February 1915. This was their answer to the British blockade and the mining of the North Sea and was designed to discourage neutral ships from taking the risk of being sunk in British waters and to encourage passengers not to travel on British liners. Though the German measure was new and shocking to many, from the point of view of German policy it had its rationale. The British war effort depended upon continuing trade; if this trade could be interrupted, then England, whom the Germans regarded as the main stay of the Entente war effort, would be forced out of the war. The longer the war lasted, the more compelling the need for the unrestricted use of the submarine appeared to Germany's military leadership.

The German declaration of the war zone represented a real threat to America's booming trade with the Allies, but this was in fact rarely mentioned in the exchange of notes between Berlin and Washington which took place in the next two years.[5] Another issue took the center of the stage. Unrestricted submarine warfare resulted in the sinking of Allied passenger vessels and caused the death of American civilians traveling upon these ships. The names of torpedoed liners, *Arabic, Lusitania, Sussex,* run like a red thread through the records of this period. America took the position that Germany was responsible for the loss of American lives and the destruction of American property.[6] This was the doctrine of strict accountability, and it found wide popular support among the American voters. German unwillingness to recognize her accountability was a challenge to American rights and honor.

The crisis which resulted from the sinking of the *Lusitania* on May 7, 1915, with the loss of 128 American lives, led to the resignation of Secretary of State William Jennings Bryan. The *Lusitania* had been carrying ammunition, i.e., contraband, and Bryan felt that the presence of American civilians on a British liner with such a cargo could not be used as a pretext to deny the enemy the right to sink the ship. Wilson, prompted by Robert Lansing, the Under Secretary of State, took the opposite view and in this case held Germany responsible for the lives of American citizens even when they traveled upon liners owned by one of the belligerents and carrying ammunition.[7] Bryan, along with his counterparts in Berlin

---

[5] Daniel M. Smith, *The Great Departure: The United States and World War I, 1914–1920* (New York: John Wiley & Sons, 1965), p. 53.

[6] Smith, 52.

[7] Smith, 55–60.

and Vienna, thought that such an interpretation was flagrantly pro-Ally, and Bryan finally resigned on June 9, 1915, in order to take his views to the public and to work for peace. He saw no reason for Americans to travel upon the ships of the belligerents in any case and wanted the United States to take a stronger line over Britain's blockade policy and thus to maintain what he considered true neutrality. Colonel Edward Mandell House and Lansing had more influence on Wilson than did Bryan.

The particularly sharp and contemptuous report about Bryan and his activities which Ambassador Dumba dispatched to Vienna reveals how little Bryan's intentions were understood by those who had the most to gain from his efforts. Dumba's reaction to Bryan was also probably due to the fact that Bryan had misinformed Dumba when he told him that the very strongly worded Allied note to the German government about the *Lusitania* was framed for domestic consumption.[8] Dumba's report of Bryan's views had led the Central Powers to underestimate the seriousness of the American attitude. However, his reaction was also conditioned by his skepticism about American neutrality, which seemed to him to serve as a cover for America's active support of the Entente. Dumba's contempt for Bryan and for all things American was destined to lead to his expulsion from the United States when his direct involvement in a campaign of industrial sabotage became known. His place was taken by the chargé d'affaires, Erich Freiherr Zwiedenek von Südenhorst, who served until the arrival of Dumba's replacement, Count Tarnowski, on the eve of the suspension of relations between the United States and the German Empire in February 1917. Zwiedenek was an extremely shrewd observer and gives the impression of having a better grasp of the American mentality than did Dumba.

The British reaction to Bryan's departure is of interest. In

---

[8] Smith, 57.

his report of June 22 to Sir Edward Grey, the Foreign Secretary, Sir Cecil Spring-Rice concluded:

One consequence of the appearance of Mr. Bryan as head of the opposition to the President must be that the latter will be bound to show an equally firm front to both parties in the European struggle in order to show his absolute impartiality. No doubt a demand will be made that all nations who commit breaches of international law must be brought to book as severely as has been the case with Germany.[9]

Four days later Colville Barclay, reporting to Sir Edward Grey for Sir Cecil, gave a further account of Bryan's activities. The fact that Bryan's talks before "German sympathizers" had made him the "hero of the German element of the population" was viewed as sourly by Britain's official representatives. A report that he was to attend a meeting of the American Neutrality League, which opposed the export of munitions by American industry, was particularly disquieting.[10] Ambassador Dumba had as little sympathy for Bryan as did the British. He does not seem to have comprehended the fact that Bryan had tried to persuade Wilson to follow a more evenhanded policy toward the Central Powers.

Negotiations continued between Washington and Berlin until the death of two Americans that occurred when the White Star liner *Arabic* was sunk on August 19. As a result of the renewed uproar in the United States, Chancellor Bethmann Hollweg, who was unable to agree to suspending submarine warfare, did promise that German submarines would sink passenger liners only after the passengers had been given time to enter lifeboats.[11] The Americans were not satisfied with this promise, and relations with Germany continued to deteriorate. The low point was reached when a German submarine torpedoed the French channel boat *Sussex* on March 24, 1916—an incident which did not in fact involve the death of any Americans. Though Wilson had no desire for war, the

[9] F.O. 371/25001/XC 7889.
[10] F.O. 371/2590/7892.
[11] Smith, 62-63.

American note (April 18) to Berlin was extremely sharp and demanded that the Germans cease "unrestricted" submarine warfare.[12] Despite strong feelings about the unfair policies pursued by America, Berlin promised in a formal note issued on May 4, 1916, to suspend attacks by submerged submarines upon merchant craft, but the German Foreign Office made it clear that they expected the United States to bring pressure to bear upon Britain to recognize the freedom of the seas.[13]

It is interesting that during the period of prolonged negotiations between Germany and the United States, which as far as the Germans were concerned was a period in which America's partiality for the Allied cause was clearly demonstrated, the British ambassador was deeply discouraged over the course of American policy. Spring-Rice's letter to Lord Robert Cecil the Deputy Foreign Secretary written on January 6, 1916, denied the frequently heard claim that England and America were uniquely and closely bound together: "For us the main thing to realize is that the majority of people here do not think so. They do not care what happens in Europe and most of them are quite indifferent to what happens to England. Many actively dislike England."[14] This led Spring-Rice to conclude: "We had better assume America is an entirely foreign country. . . . We must rely on ourselves and on our allies and not on the United States." Cecil replied comfortingly, agreeing with Spring-Rice's views. As far as Cecil was concerned it was vital to keep America from doing anything which might harm British interests. "I do not expect America to do anything for us, the utmost I look for is that she should not do anything actively against us."[15] Even for the English, dealing with the United States posed its peculiar difficulties.

---

[12] Smith, 64.
[13] Smith, 65.
[14] F.O. 371/2846/7892.
[15] F.O. 371/2846/7892.

F.O. 371/2226/XC7791
Lancelot Hugh Smith to Sir Gilbert Parker
23 WALL STREET, NEW YORK, 4th December, 1914

DEAR SIR GILBERT,

I arrived here a week ago to-day and as there have been no mails out, I have not been able to write before. I have had a good opportunity to look round and will give you my impressions.

I write from the office of J. P. Morgan & Co. where I have a private room, and they give out that I am here for their London firm. J. P. Morgan has been of the greatest service to me, both in giving me advice, asking people to meet me and telling me what he hears. They have a luncheon here every day to which they nearly always have guests of importance, and the conversation is led up to subjects which will be of interest to me. This facilitates my meeting such people in a natural manner in a way which I had not hoped for.

Morgan has a man in his office whose business it is to watch the trend of newspaper opinion for them. He assured me that he was a man of the utmost discretion and absolutely loyal to him and to England, and he has placed him entirely at my disposal.

He gets me all the papers you advised me to read daily, and also cuttings from all over the continent. As these are sent to him direct, I attract no attention. Morgan also says he will be able to procure for me the trend of opinion from any quarter I may desire. I feel this greatly assists my work, and from being able to discuss what I hear with Morgan in the evening, I can get very often both sides of the question.

I will now go through the different points of interest which I think you will care to hear.

General sentiment. Everyone I meet has no doubt as to the final issue of the war, though many think it may last a long time, and I am astounded at the feeling for the Allies and the bitterness against the Germans. I met at luncheon yesterday Mr. Strong, the President of the Federal Reserve Bank (the Govt. Bk. which is to try and take the place of the Bank of England in New York). He was asked if he noticed any change in the pro-ally feeling which there undoubtedly was at the beginning of the war. He replied. There is a great change. The feeling has increased immensely. At the commencement the feeling was largely due to the Belgian atrocities, but people had begun to consider whether when a vast haard [*sic*] of soldiers were let loose in an enemies [*sic*] country, their own country was entirely responsible for their actions, any more than a nation at peace is for the many terrible things which happen among her people, but "he said the devastation of Belgium and the dropping of bombs into unfortified towns had greatly added to the feeling here. The only important financial house here who is pro-German is Kuhn Loeb & Co., one of the most influential houses here, but then they are Jews, and you will know the feeling about Jews here, and Otto Kahn who certainly is their 2nd most important partner is a British subject and avowedly pro-British. . . . "

.   .   .   .   .

§   This is an official document, not a private report.

F.O. 371/2558/7892
                                  [*Report of Tour of G. M. Trevelyan*]
                                              SECRET
                    REPORT OF OBSERVATIONS MADE ON TOUR IN
                    THE UNITED STATES (EAST AND MIDDLE-WEST)
                              (April 12th–May 22nd, 1915)

My only *public* activity was lecturing on *Serbia* and the Austrian and Balkan questions. I did this at Universities, City Clubs, Literary Clubs, and at drawing-room meetings to collect funds for Serbian relief. The way had been prepared by Professor Pupin, the inventor and Serb Consul, a man of great ability, and by Madame Gruitch, whose eloquence had stirred up much feeling for Serbian relief. Committees for Serbian relief existed at New York, Boston and a dozen smaller places, and the Rockefeller Foundation funds were being liberally used to fight disease in Serbia. The fact that American doctors were dying of typhus in Serbia created generous competition to go out there among the doctors and medical students of the Universities. American help has been an important factor in saving Serbia from destruction by typhus. My statements about Magyar oppression in Austria-Hungary and about the Austro-Hungarian atrocities in Serbia were not challenged, though I put them into the papers as well as into my lectures. There is no strong Austrian or Magyar party in America (as distinct from German). Immigrants from Austria-Hungary—Croats, Serbs, Slovaks and Czechs are all strongly pro-ally. I saw their leaders at Chicago and New York. These various branches of the Slav race are drawing together and being organized politically to counteract the German vote. They voted solid against the German candidate at the Chicago Municipal Election and helped to secure his unexpected defeat. The majority of the Poles, including the Russian Poles, are also pro-ally. Sir Cecil Spring Rice emphasises the importance of creating political consciousness among the Slavs of America, to counteract the German vote and influence. It is beginning.

The people best able to give advice on Russian and Slav questions in the United States are Mr. Samuel N. Harper of Chicago, formerly of Liverpool University, who knows Russia well; Dr. Bianckini, Croat leader, 3207 Indiana Avenue; J. F. Stepina, President American State Bank, 1825-7, Blue Island Avenue, Chicago, Bohemian. These three work together at Chicago. At New York, Professor Pupin, Serb Consul, is the able Serb leader.

The Italians and Greeks are pro-ally. The Jews are divided but mostly anti-Russian. The Irish are divided, but mostly pro-ally in view of Home Rule; in Chicago they began as pro-ally, but the Germans got at the Bishop and a change for the bad has taken place in consequence. But taking America as a whole the Irish are pro-ally, although the division in their ranks causes them to keep rather quiet about the war. At Toronto I was told they were enlisting well in Canada, better than the French.

I did not go south of Washington, but everyone said *The South* was the most solidly pro-English part of America, as the English race is in larger proportion there than elsewhere. The *Far West* was described by persons coming thence as less interested in the war, but pro-ally—apart from the Japanese question.

The Germans themselves are not all pro-German. An important minority, chiefly consisting of "forty-eighters," viz., General Liberals who sought refuge in America from the reaction of 1849, are against the Kaiser, or on the hedge. These, and a good many Jews, have been recently deeply affected by the atrocities, submarining, etc., and tend increasingly to go with the American nation. The "hyphenated Americans" (pro-German Germans) are a body formidable out of proportion even to their great numbers, on account of their organization. But this organization and "hyphenated" attitude has much irritated the American public. They were cowed by the outburst of national wrath over the "Lusitania," and many of them publicly declared they would stand by America in case of war. If Wilson had from August last taken an openly pro-ally attitude and drifted into war with Germany out of sympathy for our side, he would have had terrible internal trouble, as the Germans are highly organized, and would in such a case have had some sympathy from the nation at large. But if Germany now forces Wilson into a war on the submarining question the Germans themselves will be divided in feeling and the rest of the country will be united behind Wilson.

Besides seeing something of the Slav leaders, I lived constantly for six weeks with leading University men, journalists, politicians and business men of the East and Middle West.* The opinions expressed in this report as to American sentiment are the residuum of some hundreds of conversations with persons of these classes.

The Universities are solid for the Allies. Nine-tenths of the Faculties (professors and lecturers) are strongly anti-German. This is remarkable, because so many of them have finished their education in Germany, but these are the loudest against her; the "pro-German" is a marked man in the American University to-day. They all declare, and I believe truly, that Germany will be academically boycotted after the war. The movement against German domination in learning and intellect had begun before the war, owing to the discovery by scientific and historical people in America that more original work was being done in these subjects in countries other than Germany. And now the war has caused American academicians to regard the German Universities as fountains of moral evil. It is greatly to be hoped that after the war the English Universities will take advantage of this opportunity to cement the intellectual and moral alliance of the Anglo-Saxon race by offering facilities for post-graduate courses which are not now available, and by welcoming and catering for our "cousins" in a less parochial spirit than has sometimes formerly obtained.

The anti-German feeling in the faculties of the Universities is just as marked at Chicago and Wisconsin Universities as it is in the East,

---

* Viz, Boston, Harvard, New York, Washington, Princeton, Yale, Philadelphia, Chicago, Wisconsin (Madison) and Michigan (Ann Arbor)—and Toronto.

although Chicago and Wisconsin are centres of German population outside the walls of these Universities.

The same remarks apply to the business men. The City Club of Chicago is just as pro-ally as the City Club of Boston, so far as I could judge from the reception of my lecture and from what the members told me about the opinion of their class. Only at Chicago the large element of German population in the classes below has caused the Chicago Press to remain neutral, and in some cases to incline slightly towards Germany contrary to the real convictions of the editors and writers.

The intensity of feeling in America about the war is remarkable. Social intercourse is rendered difficult between the two sides, and the Germans in the upper class complain of ostracism. Several persons told me that they could not do their work well from anxiety about the issue of the war. During the worst period of trade depression last winter Americans continued to subscribe millions after millions of dollars to the Belgian and other Allied Relief Funds. In many cases people sold their motor cars, refrained from investing their earnings and otherwise lived on a lower scale in order to contribute to Belgian, French, British or Serbian relief. There was, therefore, some bitterness of feeling expressed at the charge made in some English papers that America was "thinking only of the dollars." I was asked whether, if two States of the Union had been ravaged by an insolent foe, the British public would have subscribed as generously to their relief. As to the women, sewing for the war and organising of relief was as common in many parts of America as in England itself.

There are two currents of pro-ally sympathy —

1. Pro-English feeling.
2. Anti-German feeling.

No. 1 is always accompanied by No. 2, but No. 2 is also found by itself among persons contemptuous of or slightly inimical to England. These persons have become violently anti-German solely as a result of the Germans' conduct in Europe and in America since July last. The Germans were not unpopular prior to the war. They are intensely unpopular now. But hatred of modern German methods does not in all cases imply friendliness to England, and this must be borne in mind. If we presume upon the German unpopularity to do whatever we like we shall promptly arouse feeling against ourselves.

Nevertheless, the attempt of the Germans to stir up feeling against British "navalism," which was in a fair way to succeed a few months ago, has been temporarily defeated by the German submarine policy. The maritime events of the last few months, culminating in the sinking of the "Lusitania," with its sensational appeal to American humanitarian sentiment, has shown the average American that there are worse things possible than British supremacy at sea. The very fact that our supremacy is for the first time seriously challenged has shown them its value as the only safeguard of that pacific isolation which it is their national ideal to preserve. They will not kill us to make Tirpitz King.

At the same time, the pro-English sentiment (apart from the new anti-German feeling) is stronger than ever among those of English descent and those who have been brought up on English literature and thought. The present danger to England, and the sense that the Anglo-Saxon element in the United States is now a minority there, combine to make the older type of American passionately pro-English. Indeed, those whose fathers were brought up in the anti-English tradition dating from 4th of July sentiment, are now the most passionately pro-English. Senator Cabot Lodge in himself illustrates this change.

It follows that there is a good prospect of increasingly close understanding between Great Britain and the United States, and Canada and the United States in the 20th Century—an understanding, the importance of which it is impossible to exaggerate from the point of view of the survival of jeopardised Anglo-Saxon ideals in the world of to-morrow. The three elements in favour of this closer understanding are (1) the increased feeling for England in the most influential part of the population; (2) the fear of German world-domination affecting the great majority of the population; (3) the desire, now partly conscious to shelter their pacific institutions behind the British fleet. The consciousness of their own weakness has recently been borne in upon them by events.

It is greatly to be desired that our press will not begin to jeer at America if there is any disappointment about Wilson's action. People in the United States are very sensitive to English criticism, which is often barbed by over-zealous American residents in England, out of touch with the main currents of American feeling. Also, any further encroachments on international law on our part might easily revive the cry against "British navalism" in a formidable manner. For there is much criticism of England, some not at all friendly, even among those who are at present still more angry with Germany.

The great majority of the nation is anti-German, but the majority of this majority does not want to fight. European entanglements are opposed to their oldest national tradition, and war is repugnant to their present temper. Because they wish us well, but do not want to fight, they readily believe the assertion that they are doing us most good by keeping out of the war owing to the munitions question. The theory, whether true or false, suits them to a nicety.

For this reason, the export of ammunition is very popular, and is regarded by most Americans as their "contribution" to the cause of justice in Europe. It is, besides, a great and increasing vested interest, and the recovery of prosperity since the winter is attributed largely to "war orders" from the Allies. I do not, therefore, think that the German efforts to have the export stopped in order to "shorten the war" are at all to be feared. Whether competing orders from the United States Government will be a danger in the near future is another question.

The outburst over the "Lusitania" was terrific for a few days. The President might have made war if he had wished. The *Bryce Report* appearing the day after the news of the "Lusitania" received absolute credence. Till then there had been much scepticism as to the systematic character of the outrages, but Lord Bryce's name and the coincidence of the "Lusitania" outrage silenced all expressions of doubt in America, except in German circles. The use of poisoned gases added to this general impression of German barbarism.

Many of our warmest friends, who are often of a Pacifist tendency at bottom (I am not referring to Mr. Roosevelt), argue that we cannot hope to dominate the sea throughout the coming century, in view of the inventions that will be made in weapons of war, submarines, long-distance guns, etc., etc. Therefore, they say, we should consent to "neutralize the sea." But they have not clearly thought out what they mean, and it is difficult to bring them to a definition. America would strongly support general disarmament by sea and land, partly from general benevolence, and partly because she sees that she must otherwise have a large fighting force herself, which she does not wish.

PERSONALITIES

Mr. Roosevelt has no real weight at present. For reasons of internal politics, the feeling against him in the Taft section of the Republican party is very strong, and as this is the most pro-English part of the community — viz., the upper classes in the East — he is not followed by those who most agree with his strong pro-ally attitude. Also his method of attacking Wilson has been resented, even by those who themselves grumble against Wilson as weak about the war. Mr. Roosevelt is still personally popular, for he has just won a political libel action which he told me he expected to lose, — but as a political leader he is at present out of the running. He told me that he did not disapprove of Wilson's note, but that if he had been President he would have seized the German ships in the ports and only given them up when Germany has yielded to his demands. He said he did not expect there would be war with Wilson in, but if there was he intended to raise a brigade and go to fight with it in Flanders.

Mr. Taft, whom I saw, is friendly to us. He lined up behind Wilson at the "Lusitania" crisis, sending Wilson a letter of support. This action was popular.

I saw the principal members at the Administration at Washington and heard much about them both from Sir Cecil Spring-Rice, and from others. *No one* in the Cabinet is pro-German, and the best information reports that all are privately pro-English. The two ablest members, LANE and GARRISON do not conceal their sentiments in private conversation. GARRISON, the Minister for War, is a very able man. DANIELS, Secretary for the Navy, is not able, although it is quite untrue that he is pro-German. BRYAN takes little or no part in affairs. Forty-eight hours after the "Lusitania" news was published, he put it into the papers that *it was quite untrue that he has had any communication with the President!* Mr. Bryan is a Pacifist first and foremost, and as pro-ally as is consistent with that.

The President's son-in-law, MR. McAdoo, is said by some well-informed persons to be financially at the mercy of a German Bank and to be secretly serving Germany. This is, however, strenuously denied by intimates of the Wilson family, one of whom, MR. CRANE, of New York, talked to me on the subject at some length.

MR. CRANE, who is WILSON's personal friend and a strong pro-ally, was at Washington during the "Lusitania" crisis, and saw the members of the Administration intimately at that time. He came to see me off on board the "St. Paul," and told me the following facts: that the news arrived on Friday, that WILSON saw no one at all, not even a member of his Cabinet, until Monday, by which time he had made up his mind what he was going to do. He spent Saturday playing golf and walking about alone, and Sunday "with his God," being a very religious man, as Mr. Crane knows. Doubtless, also, he read the newspapers, for like Lincoln, he thinks he ought not to go far in front of or far behind public opinion. But he takes no *personal* advice, either from his colleagues, his relations, or his friends. He is a very lonely man in the White House, especially at important junctures. No one, American or foreign, enjoys free and intimate entry to him, not even Sir Cecil Spring-Rice, who appears to be on very friendly and easy terms with the rest of the Administration. He has made a rule to see no foreigners till the war is over, so I did not see him. He does not talk about the war even in his family. But all agree he is pro-Ally at heart.

The Administration was much mortified by the German Embassy's intrigues and insolence, even before the "Lusitania," and Sir Cecil's opposite line of conduct has been much appreciated by contrast. So also has his policy of preventing Englishmen from coming over to conduct propaganda against Germany, in contrast to the Dernburg methods. (My lectures on Serbia were resented by no one, because I said nothing about Germany in them.) The only thing complained of was the British censorship; various stories of its misdeeds were going about among American journalists, whether true or not I cannot say.

Wilson rallied the whole country to him by his Note; till then he seemed to be losing ground, especially with the strong pro-Ally section which was mainly Republican. But when I left they were all with him from shore to shore.

G. M. TREVELYAN

WELLINGTON HOUSE, BUCKINGHAM GATE
June 4th, 1915

§   Despite the war in Europe, America's role as a Pacific power was never far from the minds of diplomats stationed in Washington, as Dumba's letter below reveals.

PA XXXIII 52, folio 64
Subject: The command of the Pacific Ocean.
     [*The k.u.k. Ambassador C. Dumba to*]
     His Excellency, the Minister of the k.u.k. House
     and of External Affairs Stephan Baron Burian
No: 13/pol. A-C   WASHINGTON, 12 March, 1915

   The American Congress recessed last week without voting on the Jones Bill, concerning granting autonomy to the Philippines in preparation for their eventual independence. Although President Wilson used his own personal influence to bring about the passage of the bill, his efforts were in vain. The House and the Senate wasted their time with dilatory tactics and did not debate the measure.

   Rumors have appeared recently in the press, that Japan considered buying the Philippines from the United States. This might well be seen as an unsuccessful attempt by the Japanese government to pressure the American Congress. The efforts of the President to avoid a conflict with Japan by releasing the Philippines seem very understandable. Despite their present engagement in China, the Japanese are also developing an extremely lively presence in the neighborhood of the Panama Canal. Merchant ships report that no less than five Japanese battleships cruise near the canal and that they use the island of Tahiti, which belongs to France, as a base. It is reported that the Japanese have already settled there quite comfortably. As the French ambassador said some time ago, his government assigns great importance to this island as a coaling station, because it lies halfway between the Panama Canal and Australia. It is indeed questionable whether Japan will release this very important base after the war.

   Japan now possesses a series of strategic positions in the Pacific Ocean, which extend in the form of a half circle around North America, from the Kurile Islands near the Bering Straits to Tahiti in the neighborhood of the Central American waters. Japan's naval supremacy between the Bering Straits and the Malacca Channel is today an already established fact, which is accepted as such here in America, though with regret. For this reason the outlook of imperialistic circles has changed decisively during recent months. The leader of the Imperialists, Roosevelt, who only recently demanded unlimited command of the whole Pacific Ocean, has taken the changed situation fully into account in one of his published articles. Now he only demands supremacy over the eastern portion of the Pacific Ocean for the United States, while he acknowledges that the whole western portion which washes against the shores of Asia belongs to Japan's sphere of influence. As far as the Philippines are concerned he refers with resignation to the position taken by the present administration. The spheres of influence of the two empires [*Reiche*] are separated by the high seas which remain open to all nations.

The Seaman's Bill which has recently become law contains regulations governing the crew of American steamers, which makes competition with Japanese shipping hardly possible anymore for the shipping companies of the United States. As the "New York Herald" very pertinently observes this law can operate in no other way than in the sense of providing a privileged status for Japanese shipping in the Pacific Ocean. The largest American shipping company in the Pacific Ocean, the "Pacific Mail," has already decided to go out of business and the Dollar Company has reached a decision shameful to the United States: to have their ships sail under the Chinese Flag.

The federal government observes the deepest silence about developments in the Far East. However as I have learned privately, the governing circles of this country seek to console themselves by the fact that the Russo-Japanese antagonism, which existed until 1910, and which was considered as the surest guarantee for peace in the Pacific Ocean, may now again be revived as a result of the entry of the Japanese into Northern Manchuria. This may actually be true, but above all one has to consider the possibility that Russia may have lost her freedom of action in the Far East for many years.

The course of events in Southeast Asia has been extremely worrisome for Holland. Due to their common interests in the Pacific Ocean, the Dutch saw that should there be a European war, the United States was the surest guarantor for their extraordinarily rich colonies in the Far East, which the Japanese have long desired. But now, under the force of circumstances, the United States has surrendered the whole of the Asiatic basin of the Pacific to Japan. Confidential reports reaching the German ambassador here from Japan designate China as well as the Southeast Asian islands — the Philippines and the Dutch Colonies — as the countries whose acquisition the Japanese seek during the course of the present war.

The Dutch government, wisely foreseeing coming events, had invited the United States immediately after the outbreak of the war to take steps to maintain the territorial *status quo* in the Pacific Ocean. However the Dutch chargé d'affaires received from Under-Secretary of State Lansing a completely childish answer which was very typical of those who are presently in power: "the State Department has no interest in East Asian affairs; it is fully occupied aiding the return home of American tourists who have been stranded in Europe." It would have been easier for the United States to prevent England from drawing Japan into the war with a timely protest in London, than for Germany to have its suggestion that the Pacific Ocean be neutralized for the duration of the present war reach Tokyo through the American government. By a failure which can never again be made good the United States has given up its most vital interests in the Pacific Ocean vis-à-vis the yellow race, as well as those of European culture which she represented there. For this the United States must bear the full responsibility before posterity.

§   The Evidenzbureau report of a speech by President Elliot of Harvard to a gathering of Baptist ministers in Boston follows. It is interesting to note that Elliot was identified correctly but that the Baptist ministers were referred to as "Baptist priests" (*Baptistenpriester*).

5622 Evidenzbureau (Intelligence Section)
Evidenzbureau of the k.u.k. General Staff
18 April, 1915

Press Summary: ... "Do not pray for peace. I can imagine no greater catastrophe for the people of Europe than peace at the present time. Germany would retain Belgium and militarism would be victorious; peace would be a triumph for Germany after she has committed the greatest crime against a peaceful people. I cannot understand how thinking Americans can remain neutral. Freedom and all the American ideals are being desecrated in this struggle." When a priest asked President Elliot when one would be able to pray for peace, he answered him, "When Germany has been forced back into her own territories and compelled to pay Belgium complete indemnification."

Ambassador Dumba to Count Burián
Subject: Rumors concerning a Japanese base in Baja California.
27 April, 1915

[Rumors had been reported that the Japanese were setting up a coaling station in Turtle Bay. The *Los Angeles Times* reported that 4,000 troops were ashore, but this had been denied by the Navy Department. The Navy Department later admitted that Japanese ships were in the area and that American naval vessels had been sent to investigate their presence. The United States government was trying to play down the affair as a "harmless affair."]

Nevertheless the most recent report of an attempt by the Japanese to establish themselves on the West Coast of Mexico has made a deep impression here. For years the specter of the acquisition by Japan of a coaling station for its fleet in Lower California has haunted public opinion in this country. It led to the passing of a Senate Resolution in 1912 which at the time was described as an extension of the well-known Monroe Doctrine. The resolution stated in principle that the United States could not tolerate settlements on the American continent, not only on the part of foreign governments but also by organizations which were closely connected with foreign governments. At that time Magdalena Bay was the object of concern and the resolution was caused by talk of the sale of estates there to a syndicate which included several Japanese. [The report continued that the Japanese had been in Turtle Bay for months and had violated Mexican sovereignty. It also noted the cruise of a Japanese squadron down the Pacific Coast of Central America in the fall of the previous year.]

These measures taken by the Japanese Naval authorities appear quite comprehensible when one considers Japan's aspiration to appear as the leading maritime power in the Pacific Ocean. A small demonstration is alone sufficient to nip in the bud any desire on the part of the American government to act more energetically on behalf of the China. [Dumba noted that the Panama Canal was defended by a force of 5,000 infantry, and he also noted the government's reluctance to sanction an increase of naval strength in the area.] To avoid stirring up further an already aroused public opinion, the weak federal government has so far opposed all such measures.

PA XXXIII 52, folio 218
> *[The k.u.k. Ambassador C. Dumba to]*
> *His Excellency, the Minister of the k.u.k. House*
> *and of External Affairs, Stephan Baron Burian*

Subject: Mr. Bryan's remarks to the press about "the needless war."

No. 27/B   LENOX, MASS., 23 June, 1915

It was to be expected that Mr. Bryan, for whom notoriety has become an absolute necessity of life, would use the freedom which he has regained to make various written and oral pronouncements. First he published three long-winded articles entitled "The Needless War," which were only partially printed even by one of the New York papers which is favorable to him.

In the first article the apostle of freedom describes pompously the horror of war and the sacrifices with which the neutral states have been burdened. He stresses the fact that the fine task of mediating peace falls to the United States, which must lead the way by providing the example of patience and self-restraint; the greatest role which has ever come to anyone in History, that of the peacemaker, belongs to President Wilson.

In the second article, the former Secretary of State, to whom European conditions have always remained a book with seven seals, tried to prove that the World War was neither a racial, nor a religious, nor a dynastic struggle, but rather the result of a completely false philosophy of life. Its principle was "power takes precedence over right." Readiness for war had quite logically brought on the war.

Finally, in the last article Mr. Bryan stated that the nations did not know why they fought each other; each nation claims to be fighting for its existence, its way of life, and, certainly against its will, to repulse foreign aggression. It is the duty of the warring sovereigns to declare openly now what peace conditions they would accept and to transfer the responsibility for the continuation of the murderous struggle to their opponents. In conclusion Mr. Bryan pleads for his *idee fixe*. [He advocates] peace treaties based upon an obligatory investigation by a mutually acceptable international commission, which because it will sit for one year, offers the best guarantee for calming tempers and the peaceful settlement of every question at issue.

The articles of the democratic tribune of the people were hardly noticed in the New York Press. The editors of the great New York papers, who are members of the "Associated Press," even proposed that Mr. Bryan, who has announced a new statement for every coming day, be completely boycotted. This suggestion was carried out systematically only by a few papers. However the utterances of the democratic tribune of people are much too long and diffuse, oratorically ornate and repetitive of a few known favored ideas, to have been able to find particular approval with the general public. Mr. Bryan must blame his failure only upon himself and his boundless vanity.

On the 19th of this month he came to New York to figure as the main speaker for peace at a meeting of the "Central Federated Union." According to a Democratic newspaper only 1,900 people, mostly Socialists, appeared in Carnegie Hall, which seats 3,100. The English Socialist Meyer would have been greeted with greater applause than the former Secretary of State. The latter, contrary to his habit, made a rather polemical speech in which he attacked Roosevelt as well as Mr. Taft; the former as a chauvinist, who openly favors American militarism and agitates for war with Germany; the latter because he wishes to use the "League to ensure peace," which he has proposed, to enforce peace through the organization of an international police force. In conclusion Mr. Bryan condemned the agitation of bellicose newspaper editors, whom he said ought to be sent to the front along with bankers and profiteers.

This criticism was very ill received by many newspapers and consequently they completely ignored Mr. Bryan's speech, which was felt most sorely by the latter. Next Thursday the tireless abdicator desires to proclaim once again the gospel of peace at a great open air gathering in Madison Square, which has been called by German sympathizers. The appearance of Mr. Bryan hand in hand with German-Americans, workers, delegates of the peace movement and Eastside Jews, who are now all being mobilized, will not increase his popularity. He must find a new platform and new slogans before the beginning of the presidential campaign, if he wants to appear before the voters with any hope of success.

The k.u.k. Ambassador, C. DUMBA

§ The following selections reveal clearly the problems which the representatives of the Central Powers faced when dealing with the United States.

PA XXXIII 52 folio 244–246
Dumba to Burián
Subject: The Austro-Hungarian note concerning the export of war material
No. 34 pol.   LENOX, MASS., 8 August, 1915

[The version of the note published in the United States was based on cable reports from London.] Entirely contrary to custom here the State Department did not make available the full text of our protest to the Press. [Dumba had the full text translated into English by the Pressbureau of the Austro-Hungarian General Consulate in New York.] There was strong resistance to the publication of the same in New York. . . . It was possible to assure our protest the desired publicity only by a roundabout way through Washington and by bringing in other news correspondents, as well as by direct negotiations with major newspapers.

The American Press's as well as the State Department's limited cooperation with us has again revealed itself most crassly in this affair. I have the honor to present the pertinent report of the New

York Sun. It published the note with the commentary issued by the State Department that the full text could not have been made public earlier because the coded telegram with which Mr. Pennfield had sent the text of our protest arrived here garbled. It is [quite] remarkable what childish subterfuges are used here in order not to admit openly the obvious ill will towards us.

On this occasion I wish to note that the sympathy of the k.u.k. government which your Excellency expressed to Mr. Pennfield in connection with the Eastland catastrophe was hardly mentioned at all in the American Press.

PA XXXIII 52 folio 238
Dumba to Burián
Subject: The American Press reaction to the Fall of Warsaw.
No. 34/pol B   LENOX, MASS., 8 August, 1915

Many American newspapers follow the English Press so loyally that they now even serve up to their readers the stupid fairy tale that, in view of the Russian Army's successful retreat while still intact, the loss of Warsaw and the Weichsel (Vistula) line are strategically unimportant and meaningless. That it is crass nonsense to speak of a Russian Army which is still intact after the loss of 700,000 to 800,000 prisoners and as many dead and wounded, might well be evident, even to some sly Yankee. . . .

§   In the report below, the president of the Reichsbankdirectorate, Rudolf von Havenstein, answered a question that had been raised at the beginning of July as to whether or not it would be possible to purchase the stock held by Germans in American firms. The idea was that by becoming a major stockholder it would be possible for the German government to influence the policies of American corporations, in order to keep war material out of the hands of the enemy. A member of the Prussian Landtag, Fuhrman, had passed on a similar suggestion relayed to him by the editor of *Der Deutsche*

Kulturträger (The German Culture Bearer) a Grand Haven,
Michigan, newspaper. The editor, Herr Minuth, had advised
the German government to influence English-language newspapers through subventions and had proposed buying up
American firms to keep munition supplies away from the
English. Herr Minuth had told the German government, in-
correctly as it turned out, that they could gain control of
Bethlehem Steel. His suggestions were, however, investigated
and rejected on the grounds that it was impossible to purchase Bethlehem Steel. The Reichsbankdirectorate took a
similar view, as the following report will show, but it is
interesting to note that on September 10, 1915, the German
military attaché Franz von Pappen, the future Chancellor,
reported from Washington with regret that the purchase of
the Union Metalic Cartridge Co. had failed because it was
leaked to the public. He attributed this failure to pressure
from the Morgan interests.

German Foreign Ministry 21/380

BERLIN, 21 August 1915

[The report began by stating that much German-owned stock had
already been sold and that the remainder owned by Germans was
deposited in London banks. Therefore it was a real question whether enough stock could be gathered together to make a difference.]
Doubts along these lines are all the more justified, because the
largest American firms which come into question are under the
controlling influence of the Morgan group which is active in the
interest of England, and not only finances deliveries to her but also
has a deciding voice in the granting of contracts. [The report concluded by noting that German influence on the policies of major
American firms might cause legal complications because Germany
would require the firms in question to act against their best interests.]

§ A final report issued on September 16, 1915, by von
Havenstein mentioned two additional difficulties. Even if the

German government should be able to gather enough stock, it would be very hard for it to find men who could represent them upon the American boards of directors. There was also a practical problem. Even if representatives were found, it was difficult to say how stock certificates could be put in their hands.

PA XXXIII 52 folio 256–259
Report, Dumba to Burián

25 August, 1915
...In view of the information which I have received I am convinced that despite our outstanding military success the present moment is not favorable for beginning negotiations for a loan. . . .

§   Submarine warfare occupied everyone's attention by the late summer of 1915.

The following report concerns the danger of war with America. The Royal Bavarian military plenipotentiary, General Freiherr von Nagel zu Aichberg, reported to his government.[16]

M. Kr. 1829
*Royal Bavarian Military Plenipotentiary to
The War Minister*
Subject: Special Report

No. 4317   GHQSM   9.8.15

...The danger of war with America no longer exists. . . . A great

---

[16] The larger German federal states, Saxony, Württemberg, and Bavaria, had military as well as civilian representatives both at German Supreme Headquarters and at Berlin. The reports which these representatives sent back to their respective governments are often most revealing. It is worth noting in passing that the German federal states, especially Bavaria, also had war aims of their own. These have been discussed in Karl-Heinz Janssen's *Macht und Verblendung*.

deal of theatrical thunder against England has been staged in the United States; I believe that they threaten each other with friendly understanding, in order to simulate neutrality. . . .

Our submarine warfare will be continued, but with the limitation that for the time being large passenger liners are not to be sunk without warning. That is however strictly private and *top secret*!

M. Kr. 1829
Report of the Military Plenipotentiary
No. 4598   13.9.15

. . . The cases of the "Arabic" and the "Hesperian" have led to this: the Emperor has forbidden the continuation of submarine warfare in the present form; and—as I hear, at the demand of the Supreme Command—limitations have been ordered, which appear to those who are presently directing the war at sea to amount to the abandonment of submarine warfare against merchant vessels.

As a result of this Admiral von Tirpitz, Admiral Bachmann and Rear Admiral Behnke have handed in their resignations. As far as it is now known only those of the latter two will be accepted. Admiral von Tirpitz's offer to resign has not been approved, but the authority, given to him at the beginning of the war by His Majesty, to influence the conduct of the war at sea, which led to the introduction of submarine warfare against merchant ships, has been expressly taken away from him. It is not yet clear what Admiral von Tirpitz will do about this. Admiral von Holtzendorff has been named to be Bachmann's successor as Chief of the Naval Staff.

PA XXXIII 52 folio 261–265
Dumba to Burian
Subject: The question of the Arabic and the Lusitania.

LENOX, MASS., 31 August, 1915

. . . A dramatic change of feeling has taken place. [Dumba reported the reaction to the official German statement that it was not yet known whether the submarine commander had exceeded his authority.] This certainly limited and qualified concession was sufficient to produce a feeling of relaxation and the greatest satisfaction in the Washington administration, and at the same time to cause the press to peal in unison the bells of peace. Once again it has been revealed clearly how much the Cabinet and influential circles in politics, finance and commerce here tremble before a possible conflict with Germany however much they strive to give the impression by means of chauvinistic statements of a desire to fight. The Chancellor's explanations led immediately to the conclusion that instructions in the sense of the American note had already been issued to the U-boat commanders, and that the "Arabic" incident can be closed simply by disavowing and punishing the guilty commandant, as well as by offering compensation for the life of the two dead Americans. [The willingness of of the German government to make concessions on the question of the *Lusitania* also had had an effect.] Most journalists are completely satisfied with the turn of events. The Jingo newspapers speak with contempt of the "folding up" on the part of the Teutonic powers, who are usually so defiant, and they behave as if the United States had won a great victory. The more reasonable and the few decent papers congratulate the President on his moderation and firmness which has made possible a satisfactory settlement of the disputed matter.   The stock exchange greeted the German government's willingness to make concessions by a marked upward trend among the leading stocks. . . .

5622 Evidenzbureau Summary
A Report from the k.u.k. Military Attaché in Stockholm, Col. Eugen Straub[17]

2 October, 1915

According to news from New York the peace propaganda which is being carried on by German Americans and the Irish is gaining support. All English newspapers work against this propaganda and agitate for war. Still it is hoped that the peace movement will also succeed in Washington and will win Wilson for this cause.

---

[17] Straub, a colonel in the General Staff, was attaché for the Nordic nations, i.e., Norway, Sweden, Denmark. Evidenzbureau was the intelligence section of the General Staff.

§   The reason for the German government's initial caution about offending the United States is revealed by the two reports that follow. There was already alarm in official circles about Germany's dwindling reserves. The Bavarian military plenipotentiary, General von Nagel, the author of both reports, and the two pessimistic sources referred to in his first report, Quartermaster General von Freytag-Loringhoven and Colonel von Lossberg, Chief of the Operations Section, Western Theater, were all in favor of arranging a negotiated peace as soon as possible. To achieve this they believed Germany would have to give up her conquests in the West but not the East.[18]

M. Kr. 1829
                    The Royal Bavarian Military Plenipotentiary to
                                the War Minister
Subject: A report on morale.
No. 5259   GHQSM   8 November, 1915

[He had heard that there was considerable pessimism in the Foreign Office, where it was believed that the war could not go on. Therefore he found the occasion to speak with Excellency von Freytag-Loringhoven, the Quartermaster General, concerning the matter.] He [Freytag-Loringhoven] also said with reference to this that in the spring of 1916 our military strength will be exhausted, and therefore a speedy conclusion of peace is necessary. To justify this view he added that in the spring the number of officers and available men will decline and that the heavy losses of fathers of families and the domestic price increases will become unbearable. [Freytag-Loringhoven also stated that the deep involvement in the Balkans made it impossible to withdraw troops from this theater.] Therefore sufficient strength cannot be freed for an offensive in the

---

[18] Karl-Heinz Janssen, *Der Kanzler und der General: Die Führungskrise um Bethmann Hollweg und Falkenhayn, 1914–1916.* (Göttingen: Musterschmidt Verlag, 1967), 174, 188.

West and consequently this plan must be given up. It is no longer possible to reach a decision against the Entente by force and a war of attrition is unbearable over a long period of time for all parties. The war can be ended by making a peace settlement upon a reasonable basis, for which, to be sure, Germany may not officially take the initiative.... [Freytag-Loringhoven also informed him that Colonel von Lossberg, Chief of the Operations Section, Western Theater, no longer believed in the possibility of an offensive.] We Germans must be glad that with such a middling ally we have till now done so well in this war against so many enemies, and we should be satisfied with a large war reparation, the removal of Kurland and Poland (from Russia), and the adjustment of the border in Alsace-Lorraine. We should use Belgium only as collateral and an object of exchange. [The report continued that von Freytag-Loringhoven was not an official spokesman but reflected a widely held aversion to an offensive in the West. To balance this opinion von Nagel reported that the troops wanted an offensive and felt superior to the French, but he was compelled to add:] Nothing changes the fact that in the letters from the Front and from home a longing for peace is more frequently expressed. In my opinion the expression in the press of war weariness at home should be prevented by every means available, for the enemy press will exploit this to the fullest. [The plenipotentiary also stated that various army commanders in the West with their chiefs of staff believed an offensive could be carried out (durchführbar),] So that France would not indeed feel herself as the victor in the peace negotiations.... [He expressed his belief that once Serbia had been knocked out of the war, and provided there was enough ammunition, Germany was capable of a successful offensive. He also said that he hoped the Supreme Command did not share Freytag-Loringhoven's opinions.] I view it as most necessary, for the Imperial Government to put an end to the articles of some-one like Harden and of the *Vorwärts*. Otherwise the government leave themselves open—aside from the effect abroad—to the suspicion that they agree with the main outlines of their despondency. Here at the Front one notices no signs of exhaustion or lack of courage. When one meets officers and troops even after bloody fighting, one is proud of the spirit of confidence and the determination "to win"!

M. Kr. 1829
Royal Bavarian Military Plenipotentiary to
the War Minister
Subject: Report of a discussion with von Falkenhayn.

No. 5511   GHQSM   30.XI.15

It was noted with respect to the West that the war must be decided there and that this depended upon maintaining our fighting strength and the ability to hold out. To achieve this the troops must be husbanded and the demand for reserves gradually limited to the point where units remain at their establishment and not above it. . . . Unsuccessful undertakings in the West were warned against, for they had a much more dangerous effect upon morale than did even greater defeats in the East. . . .

§   The issue of submarine warfare remained a crucial one for Germany, as well as for the United States. The military technicians both in Berlin and at Supreme Headquarters were determined to have the final word. Von Nagel reported the following conference between the Chancellor, the Chief of the Naval Staff, and General Erich von Falkenhayn on March 5.

M. Kr. 1830
Royal Bavarian Military Plenipotentiary to
the War Minister
Subject: Submarine Warfare

No. 6577   GHQSM   5.3.16

A Conference between Chancellor von Bethmann Hollweg, Chief of the Naval Staff Holtzendorff and von Falkenhayn.

The Navy believes that the war can only be ended, if it becomes so unpleasant for England herself that she will be inclined to make peace. England cannot be brought this far by land warfare alone.

Therefore it is necessary to attack her with every possible means of sea and air warfare. Among these means is unrestricted submarine warfare which must cut off food supplies to England without consideration for the trade, etc., of neutrals. [The Navy believes it has enough submarines and claims that it is now time to attack because this is the time when grain is shipped to England. The Navy also hopes that the resumption of unrestricted submarine warfare will bring the British Navy to battle.] . . . and that there will then be an opportunity to inflict a decisive blow upon the English fleet.

So far his Majesty, the Emperor, has apparently not decided whether or not to accept the suggestions of the Navy. The Imperial Chancellor's and the Foreign Office's apprehensions that by waging ruthless submarine warfare we would cause America, the Nordic States and also Rumania to declare war against us and their belief that this must be avoided still provide opposition to the plans of the Navy.

I do not know what the attitude of the Chief of the General Staff is; the Minister of War, Wild von Hohenborn, whose military views the Chief of the General Staff values, is said to have expressed himself very positively in favor of a more intensive conduct of the war.

§   Two days later von Nagel sent another report on the same subject.

M. Kr. 1830
No. 6610   GHQSM   7.3.16

The discussions about submarine warfare seem to have ended and in fact in favor of the Imperial Chancellor, who maintained the view that, to begin with, Germany would win the war even without an intensification of submarine warfare. Therefore she has no reason to worsen her political position by taking measures which would lead to a declaration of war by America and in addition perhaps also that of the Nordic States. [The Emperor explained how difficult his decision was] ... that for the moment diplomatic considerations must be decisive and consequently there was to be no intensification of the submarine campaign. ... The decision called forth the expression of great regret among Naval officers, for the majority of the Navy is convinced that in the face of the relentless sinking of ships England could hold out for only a few months and in this way could be forced to make peace. [He said that Bethmann believed that peace was possible but that the chance for peace had not been taken because the statesmen who were there when the war began are still in power.] He remarked recently that these men were all the more for the continuation of the war, because they themselves were responsible for its outbreak; thus Samzonow is the one who is now the least interested in peace. In the case of Grey the Chancellor appears to assume that he really wanted to restrain Russia from war and that he had joined the declaration of war, which was provoked by Russia, only unwillingly. According to the above, because France supported Russia's behavior from the start, it is Grey who is responsible for the War. I cannot say either whether because of this, the Chancellor views him as the one most inclined to peace or whether this influences his attitude towards submarine warfare.

§   A few days later von Nagel again reported.

M. Kr. 1830

                                 Top Secret
No. 6749   GHQSM   23.3.162

So far I have been able to learn this much:

Grand Admiral von Tirpitz's dismissal was the result of his continued agitation in favor of unrestricted submarine warfare, despite His Majesty's decision. [The report then noted the background of friction between the Chancellor and von Tirpitz. Bethmann Hollweg believed that Tirpitz had tried to get rid of him. As far as the plenipotentiary was concerned, the Chancellor's previous mistrust of Tirpitz was fully justified] ... for, as I have been informed from various sources, Tirpitz always agitated secretly against the Chancellor. [The Emperor's reasons for not engaging in unlimited submarine warfare were then carefully explained] . . . we would have had to expect that neutral states, as in the case of Portugal, would have confiscated our ships and that we would have been forced to send substantial parts of our field armies against at least Holland and Denmark and thereby to weaken our other fronts. [Then he began to give a summary of the paper which the Naval Secretary had sent along to the conference] . . . that we are now in a position to carry on submarine warfare in such a way that we could sink all the . . . ships in the War Zone around England, and thereby compel her to beg for peace due to lack of food within at the most 6 months. [The conflict between Bethmann Hollweg and Tirpitz was again discussed and Tirpitz's reputation as a "strong man" (*starker Mann*) noted.] . . . without presuming to judge this most worthy man, I must quite impartially mention that his love of truth and the constancy of his opinions are not considered by all to be reliable. But one thing must be said. Tirpitz has always stood for unrestricted submarine warfare; he has also always stressed that we must say publicly we want to keep Belgium. Even if we should be compelled to give up a portion of Belgium, he believes we will still have increased its worth as an article of exchange, because we have shown that this part (of it) was also valuable to us. [He next referred to a discussion of the matter with the Emperor, who claimed that if Tirpitz had been Chancellor he would have made the same decision. The Emperor also indicated that he believed Tirpitz wanted to become Chancellor and expressed his displeasure over the Conservative resolution:] and the fact . . . that this party, whose members are frequently the fathers of officers or themselves former officers wishes at this time to interfere with the authority to command[19] and the Army High Command. [Despite Bethmann's success, von Nagel still believed that he would be replaced.] A stronger man — Falkenhayn or Dalwitz — should direct the peace negotiations. The fact that the Conservatives have never forgiven the Chancellor for his attitude on the question of the Prussian Electoral Law plays a role in this issue. The Chancellor has other opponents in the Pan-Germans who desire a greater emphasis upon and expression of the most extensive annexation plans, and in

---

[19] The *Kommandogewalt* was the Emperor's special preserve.

the National Liberals of Basserman's persuasion, who follow Tirpitz through thick and thin. It would be desirable for the Reichstag and the people to recognize that this is a most unpropitious time for internal disagreements. His Excellency von Falkenhayn expressed this view in the discussion with His Majesty after dinner which has already been referred to.

Beyond this my opinion is that the government's much discussed note to America is the chief cause of the present discontent. The note was generally viewed as a declaration of a feud: as a proclamation, that from now on Germany would be guided solely by her own interests and views in the [question] of submarine warfare and would wage it as rigorously as possible. But that was not the purpose of the memorandum. It was supposed to be a "diplomatic demarché" which sought chiefly to recapitulate once again for America the whole development of the commercial and submarine warfare question. This was done because, as time passed, the reason for this development, which was the product of necessity, was obscured in an undesirable way and falsely presented to the American public. Our people apparently have no real understanding for this kind of diplomatic subtlety and I must admit, that I only more or less understood the matter after a careful explanation. It will now be up to the Chancellor to persuade the Reichstag that we did not intend to declare unrestricted submarine warfare and then crawled back from doing so, but rather that the memorandum and what was connected with it aimed only at the above.

§ The report from Berlin to the Bavarian Minister of War by General Karl Ritter von Köppel that follows provides a brief summary of the debates on the question of submarine warfare. (*Verhandlungen der verstärkten Haushaltskommission über die U-Bootkriegsfrage*).

M. Kr. 1828
No. 2738   GHQSM   28, 29, 30 March 1916

Stresemann thinks that our false approach to Wilson dates from the day we summoned him as the *arbiter mundi* [judge of the world] in the question of the Dum-Dum bullets. It must be admitted that we have not been exactly conciliatory towards America in our notes, but rather in our deeds, which has hurt us with our friends in America. Although he viewed a breach with America as very serious, he valued much more highly than did the Chancellor the effect upon England of the loss of so much tonnage, because England's economic foundation is trade. . . . Major industrialists and bankers have been asked about this, and they consider the loss of a tonnage of 4 million, which Admiral von Capelle has described as possible within six months, sufficient to bring about England's collapse. . . . The danger of a break with America also exists with the present form of submarine warfare, as soon as a U-boat commander carelessly exceeds his instructions. . . .

§   The problem of submarine warfare continued as a subsequent report by von Köppel reveals.

M. Kr. 1830
No. 6941   GHQSM   12.IV.16

The reports of the enemy press, that we are now using a U-boat without a periscope are false. There is no such boat. The report is apparently being spread about to make it appear possible that ships can be torpedoed without the appearance of a periscope. Thus it will be possible to claim that ships which have struck mines, were illegally torpedoed by German submarines. The newspaper report that three of our U-boats are operating on the coast of the United States of America is equally incorrect for they have no base there. We do not deny these reports as they are of advantage to us insofar as the freight and insurance rates for ships sailing to England remain, as a result, very high and because the hiring of ship's crew is thereby made more difficult.

§   The Bavarian plenipotentiary reported as follows.

M. Kr. 1830
Nr. 7031   GHQSM   21.IV.16

The American note about submarine warfare is extremely un-friendly. I have yet been unable to discover how it is to be answered.

M. Kr. 1830
Nr. 7041   GHQSM   22.IV.16

The Imperial Chancellor has again departed for Berlin. Before anything further happens the full text of the American note is await-ed.

M. Kr. 1830
No. 7061   GHQSM   24.IV.16

[The report opened with an estimate of the value of German ships in American ports.] Some of the ships are very valuable. According to the price of ships before the increase in value caused by the war, the Hamburg-America Line estimates the value of its ships im-pounded in America at 200 million; the North German Lloyd at 150 million.[20]

PA XXXIII 52 folio 181–188

K.u.k. Chargé d'affaires Zwiedenek to Baron Burián
WASHINGTON, 27 April, 1916

[Zwiedenek reported Count Bernstorff's impression that the Ger-man government was inclined to make concessions on the question of submarine warfare.] With this a break can apparently be avoided at least for the moment, for it was upon just this point that Wilson's speech before Congress as well as the note to Germany seemed to turn. . . .

The true intentions of the President are unclear. Several entirely pessimistic observers, who assured me recently there was no doubt now that Wilson aimed directly at a break with Germany, are now inclined to believe that he again merely sought to gain an electoral

---
[20] Marks.

success and that he would be very happy if the means employed would result in something serious. The manner in which President Wilson behaved during the present crisis toward the German ambassador through his friend House, who sought to help Wilson in settling this matter—of course always in accordance with the outcome Wilson desired—verifies this opinion. Another view of the matter is that Wilson was not so much led by egoistic motives as by the *idée fixe* which increasingly obsesses him that he must come to the aid of England, by compelling Germany to give up the only weapon with which she might eventually be able to vanquish England. Many unbiased observers no longer believe in the sincerity of Wilson's light-headed humanitarianism. Nevertheless it is possible that through autosuggestion he himself is convinced of the nobility of his belief.

... Should there be a break with Germany, it is to be expected that a good portion of the Irish in this country, who now favor President Wilson, will turn against him. Nevertheless there can be no doubt that very influential elements in the administration are decidedly hostile to the Central Powers. This is also demonstrated by the vast apparatus which tirelessly seeks wherever possible to collect hostile information in order to discredit Germany as well as our agencies, and thereby to influence the attitude of the press. In the case of a break all possible charges that we had violated neutrality would indeed be made. [Zwiedenek then discussed the Papen Affair.] ... unfortunately through carelessness and betrayal, the officials of the Justice Department are again and again given material.

M. Kr. 1830
Secret
Von Nagel to the Minister of War
Subject: Negotiations with America.
No. 7089   GHQSM   28.4.16

From what I have been able to find out here, the intention is to send a conciliatory answer to America in which the circumstances leading to submarine warfare against merchant ships are once again explained. The answer will also provide further explanations about the Sussex and similar incidents, and again propose that Americans use only certain ships and routes in their journeys to Europe. In addition some kind of a statement which will make the members of Congress aware that the rupture of diplomatic relations would lead automatically to war within a very short time is contemplated. It is still assumed that the majority of the Congress did not wish to leave Wilson in the lurch after he had made public his note but nevertheless did not want war with Germany.

For military and political reasons it is desired to avoid an open conflict with America as long as is possible. First of all, from the military standpoint, we must consider that the Americans could confiscate about 500,000 tons of shipping space which would result in an enormously increased task for our submarines, if they want to interrupt England's food supply. In the second place we would be compelled to send a particularly valuable part of our own merchant fleet to the bottom of the sea, which would greatly hinder the resumption of our commerce for a long time after the end of the war. We would also have to expect that America would allow and encourage voluntary enlistment for military service against Germany, whereby as in Canada large numbers of soldiers could be recruited. Besides, American officers would provide a welcome increase for the English Army which is already suffering from a shortage of good officers. The complete harnessing of America's financial and industrial strength against us would also greatly increase our enemy's power of resistance, especially now when there indeed are some indications that the enemy's hope of victory has somewhat moderated. Politically, the danger would be that the smaller neutral nations would be subjected to such economic pressure that willy-nilly they would have to join the Entente, merely to achieve a quick end to the war. Admiral von Holtzendorff said to me yesterday that even the states friendly to us might no longer be entirely reliable should it come to war with America; Austria-Hungary has already rather emphatically expressed its aversion to war with America. I gathered from the Admiral's other remarks that he believed the further conduct of submarine warfare would have to conform to political necessity and that in any case he did not share the opinion of our Pan-Germans, etc., who demand unrestricted submarine warfare, without considering the consequences. It seems to me to come down to this: the responsible imperial officials agree insofar as it is possible upon a conciliatory attitude toward America.

Admiral von Holtzendorff also told me a few interesting details. The Admiralty still believes that we did not torpedo the Sussex and the Tubantia and that America should be told this once again. With respect to the Sussex reports are now at hand that a troop transport was sunk, in the area in question a fact which so far has been particularly carefully concealed by the enemy. Indeed our U-boat commander has reported that he did not sink the Sussex, but rather a troop transport, but so far because of the place and time of the sinking the Americans have doubted the existence of a second ship. It would of course be helpful if our Admiralty could provide evidence that a second ship was present. In addition I believe that in the case of the Sussex we will agree to let the Americans examine all the evidence and promise that we will be impartial in our examination of all the available materials in possession of the Americans which up to the present we have not been able to do because they were not available to us. As far as the Tubantia is concerned, all of our records, etc., were opened to the Dutch torpedo expert who was able to confirm that the screw allegedly found with the number printed upon it originates from a torpedo which was fired by a German submarine long before the sinking of the Tubantia and was recorded as a miss: "fired under the enemy." This torpedo was lost and we did not find or use it again. The fragment of the warhead, which has also been found, originates from a torpedo which was indeed manufactured by Schwartzkopff, but whose caliber has never been used by the German Navy and could not have been fired by us. Admiral von Holtzendorff said to me that the Dutch officer in question had stated that he himself had expected nothing else, because he had always been of the opinion that a submarine from another country had torpedoed the Tubantia. Admiral von Holtzendorff certainly did not say openly that the English torpedo neutral ships to make difficulties for us, but it seems to me that this is his opinion. In any case the Admiral appears to be certain that, despite the apparently convincing evidence in Wilson's note, we can show that we did not violate our pledge.

The report that American customs officials have been placed upon German ships interned in American ports, in order to prevent the destruction of the ships' equipment, etc., appears to be true. This gesture cannot yet be seen as directly hostile, because the measure can be justified in terms of permissible harbor policing. Nevertheless it is unfortunate for us that by doing this the Americans have made sure that our ships will fall into their hands, completely undamaged in the event of war.

It has turned out to be true that a certain amount of sabotage against American munitions factories, etc., has been carried on by our agents. It appears that several compromising documents were found on the arrested agent, Igel. The Americans are naturally once again agitated over this. Propaganda among the Irish in America is supported by the Germans.

This evening the American ambassador in Berlin, Mr. Gerard, is coming to GHQ; he is to be received by His Majesty, the Emperor. I have not yet been able to find out how this meeting was arranged: particularly whether Gerard or the Imperial Chancellor instigated it. [The rest of the letter described the failure of Casement's expedition to Ireland.]

§   Von Nagel reported Ambassador Gerard's visit, as follows.

M. Kr. 1830
               Von Nagel to the Minister of War
No. 7101   GHQSM   30.IV.16

Ambassador Gerard is said to have returned very satisfied from his journey yesterday to the care centers of the American Help Committee. I heard in passing that he is supposed to be invited to dinner with His Majesty, the Emperor, this evening. Apart from him only the Chancellor and representatives of the Foreign Office, but not the Chief of the General Staff and the Naval Staff, are said to have been invited. The latter remains here at GHQ; the Secretary of the Imperial Navy Department returns to Berlin today. I visited Excellency von Holtzendorff today at noon and gained the impression from my conversation with him and Excellency von Capelle that the Navy will make all the concessions necessary to avoid war with America, which—as Excellency von Holtzendorff said to me—we would feel very much economically and would weaken our internal power of resistance. The reply to America will probably be formulated tomorrow. . . .

§   The Emperor and the Ambassador.

M. Kr. 1830
                    Von Nagel to the Minister of War
Nr. 7121   GHQSM   1.5.16

[The Ambassador and the Emperor had lunch together after a walk in the park of the villa which lasted a half hour. Everything was said to have gone well and the Chancellor was satisfied. It had been decided not to have the Ambassador visit the Front.] . . . a journey to the trenches in the neighborhood of Rheims was viewed by the Chief of Staff as useless, because during its course unlovely remarks about American munitions and the like would be unavoidable. This evening the Ambassador returns to Berlin.

He requested the audience and in view of the present critical situation could not be refused. . .; it seems that he took away a good impression but it is not yet possible to say whether anything positive will result from it. [He does not yet know the contents of the note], still I believe that Germany will agree to consider the interests of neutrals in the conduct of submarine warfare, as she has done before, but that the continuation of this [type] of warfare is necessary for Germany.

§   Von Nagel reported Falkenhayn's last attempt to obtain the continuation of unrestricted submarine warfare.[21]

M. Kr. 1830

                    Von Nagel to the Minister of War

Subject: Friction at GHQ.

No. 7135   GHQSM   3.5.16

[Falkenhayn's desire to resign because of his difference of opinion

---

[21] Falkenhayn viewed unrestricted submarine warfare as an essential component of his own plans for the Western Front.

with the Chancellor was reported. General von Plessen had persuaded him not to resign. The Chancellor had gone to Berlin to talk
with the political parties. The report then explained what happened.]
On Sunday at the daily private briefing on the state of the war
Excellency von Falkenhayn told the Emperor that unrestricted submarine warfare against England must be continued in order to short-
en the duration of the war, even if as a result of it America should
declare war. [The Chancellor saw that the Emperor was influenced
by this statement.] The Chancellor maintained his usual position that
the entry of America into the war against us would greatly worsen
our diplomatic position and lengthen the war indefinitely, because
the enemy would draw new hope, as well as all kinds of resources
from the open hostility of America. No final decision was reached at
this briefing. [When the presence of the American ambassador required that a definite position be taken, the Emperor supported the
Chancellor and his views were expressed in the note. One reason for
this was Admiral von Holtzendorff's statement.] Excellency von
Holtzendorff expressed the opinion that it would not be unwelcome
to the Navy if a certain limitation were imposed upon submarine
warfare. [The Chancellor got the Emperor to agree to the form of the
note in von Falkenhayn's absence and without his being informed of
its contents.] . . . he felt that he had been insulted and ignored by this
action and handed in his resignation. . . . In any case there is no
evidence that the Chancellor intended to pass over Excellency von
Falkenhayn; it was an omission due to the fact that His Majesty, the
Emperor, reached a decision much more quickly than the Chancellor
had expected it.

The conflict between the Chief of the General Staff and the
Chancellor is ended; my opinion is that it will remain latent and will
be kept alive by various people here.

M. Kr. 1830

Von Nagel to the Minister of War

No. 7171   GHQSM   7.V.16

. . . According to quite reliable reports, the American ambassador,
Gerard, has described the German reply as "very clever" in conversations with American friends. . . .

PA XXXIII 52 folio 189

Chargé Zwiedenek to Burián

WASHINGTON, 6 May, 1916

[The German decision to suspend unrestricted submarine warfare had avoided a break.] An act of caution which was not absolutely necessary to avoid a break, but in view of the delicate situation does indeed appear to have been opportune. The blunt reference to the obviously partisan attitude of the United States during the whole war will somewhat limit President Wilson's pleasure over his new diplomatic victory but still he can be very much satisfied, for his position in the election campaign has been significantly strengthened and he has done a great service to the Allies, perhaps a greater service than if it had really come to a break.

It is certain that, should Wilson really be called to play the undeserved role of a peacemaker, the Central Powers could not expect from him *proprio motu* a sympathetic attitude. As far as the Allies are concerned he would where possible urge compromises in their favor.

§ Concerning Wilson's note, von Köppel reported to the Bavarian Minister of war, as follows:

M. Kr. 41

Von Köppel to the Bavarian Minister of War
Confidential

Subject: Sitting of the Budget Committee of the Reichstag.

No. 1361   6.5.1916

[First, Bethmann's speech to the committee was reported. The Chancellor believed Wilson's note was no bluff.] . . . the assumption that this is a bluff seems to me to be unlikely. The following factors appear to have caused the President to issue the note: (1) First and foremost are the considerations which affect the election. The issues of the election are so important to him that he considers a break with

Germany to be secondary to them. (2) The Lusitania and the Sussex incidents have caused a false impression among many Americans that our U-boat commanders did not seriously intend to abide by their instructions. But this is not correct. In respect to the case of the Sussex it is understandable that the Americans should imagine we torpedoed the ship. On the basis of the U-boat commander's report our Admiralty Staff still believes that we did not torpedo the Sussex. (3) It is widely believed in America that those men who represent Germany there unofficially are guilty of activities which are not permitted in a neutral country. But it is out of the question that the German Government had encouraged such behavior. (4) It is known that the money interests in Washington pursue pro-English policy.

If at this time I had advised the Emperor in favor of the suspension of diplomatic relations, this would not have meant an immediate declaration of war, but I cannot think of how it could have been long avoided; every new incident would have provided an occasion for war. . . .

The tone and contents of the note made it difficult for me to make concessions, but I can only consider a policy to be right, which is realistic and in this respect I have come to the conclusion that we must make those concessions to America which will serve to avoid a break with her. America does not demand that we give up submarine warfare; I am convinced that only a concession, which limits the submarine cruiser warfare to the war zone can avoid a break.

The situation is now this: after 21 months of war we have succeeded, not only in holding off our enemy but also in gaining for ourselves a military position, which can be described as "good." If I had presented the American ambassador with a note, which resulted in the suspension of diplomatic relations I ask in what kind of a situation would I have placed the German fatherland. I would have failed to have found a way to protect the German people from a serious threat and from a worsening of its military, industrial and financial position.

These considerations have forced me to the decision to commend to the Emperor the note in the form which has been placed before you.

It is difficult to gain an absolutely reliable picture of what Wilson actually desires and I cannot guarantee that, despite the note, the situation will not take a turn for the worse, but then the wrong will be clearly with the other side, and we can continue to defend ourselves against a world of enemies. I don't believe that Wilson merely sought a platform for his reelection and that we were supposed to provide him with it. . . .

The Imperial Chancellor then read the text of the note. Representatives of all parties spoke; all agreed with the note except the Conservatives. . . .

The efforts of private individuals such as Mr. Henry Ford to end the war were even more incomprehensible to the representatives of the Central Powers than certain aspects of President Wilson's foreign policy.

5622 Evidenzbureau

From the Military Attaché in Stockholm

29.12. 1915

News summary: Ford's American peace expedition. Reception in Norway was very cool. No one takes the undertaking seriously. The main figure in Ford's party seems to be the Hungarian Jewess, Roszika Schwimmer (an agitator for the right of the women to vote), who makes a very unpleasant impression. Henry Ford himself is an idealistic peace enthusiast.

5622 Evidenzbureau:

From the Military Attaché in Stockholm

5.5.1916

News summary: America: The Ford peace mission seems to be breaking up. The Swedish and Norwegian members have already left it as a result of a disagreement and because of the difficulty in finding the proper way to prepare peace.

CHAPTER **III**

America Becomes Involved

§   The period from May 1916 to April 1917 can be described as one in which the war became more terrible. Falkenhayn tried to wear out the French at Verdun, which led to his downfall, while Haig marched England's youth to death on the Somme in July. In the official circles of both the Entente and the Central Powers men talked of a longing for peace but sought to achieve it by the ever more complete organization of their societies for war. The struggle was soon to become too much for Russia and almost too much for Austria-Hungary.

As far as the Germans were concerned, their willingness to suspend "unrestricted" submarine warfare brought them no advantage. The ensuing months saw a tightening rather than a loosening of the British blockade. Even mail to the Central Powers was interfered with. British policy gave Wilson cold comfort, and this period marked a real low point in Anglo-American relations. Fortunately for the Allies, it also saw a great increase in the strength of the military's influence upon the German government. General von Falkenhayn, himself an unsuccessful advocate of unrestricted submarine warfare, was replaced at the end of August 1916 by Field

Marshal Paul von Hindenburg, and General Erich Ludendorff became the First Quartermaster General. Once this famous duo had established themselves at German Headquarters, the resumption of unrestricted submarine warfare was really only a matter of time. Ludendorff, who dominated Hindenburg, was a brilliant military technician and he was determined to achieve a German victory by the only means he understood, the successful employment of all of Germany's weapons. Though the façade of some kind of civilian government remained, under Hindenburg and Ludendorff Germany became a military dictatorship.

Domestic politics dominated the American scene, but the war was not forgotten. The slogan "He kept us out of war" brought Woodrow Wilson victory at the polls in November, 1916. Strengthened by a renewed mandate, Wilson sought once more to be the peacemaker Bryan had always wanted him to be. Though his advisers warned against his efforts, and in the case of Secretary Lansing probably worked against them, the rumors that Germany would resume "unrestricted" submarine warfare spurred Wilson on.[1] An apparently serious German effort to seek peace negotiations in December 1916 anticipated Wilson's efforts by a matter of days. The Allies did not accept either overture and viewed Wilson's activity with great hostility. One British observer remarked, ". . . I myself think that he had prepared it as a little Xmas gift to bring himself into the limelight." [2]

Germany resumed unrestricted submarine warfare on January 31, and America severed diplomatic relations with her on February 3, 1917. Wilson still seems to have hoped to avoid war, but the clumsy attempts of the German government to involve Mexico in an anti-American alliance (the Zimmermann Affair) and the sinking of American merchant ships brought about what was by now an almost inevitable

---

[1] Daniel M. Smith, *The Great Departure: The United States and World War I, 1914–1920* (New York: John Wiley & Sons, 1965), 71.
[2] F.O. 395/70/9285.

decision. War was declared against Germany on April 6, 1917, but a similar decision was delayed in the case of Austria-Hungary until December 1917.[3]

The views and activity of the British government in this period are of great interest. Propaganda played a vital role in winning and retaining the sympathy of the American nation. The British Government was not averse to creating difficulties for those who were able to influence public opinion and favored policies hostile to Allied needs. William Randolph Hearst was a case in point. At least from the British point of view, his papers had a way of "garbling" the "truth" and of making such outrageous statements as "The British government not only lies but knows that it lies." These and similar published statements led one British official to say, "Hearst is a yellow dog who has no code of honour. . . ." His International News Service was barred from the Official London Press Bureau in October 1916. Then, at Sir Cecil Spring-Rice's suggestion, the Canadian paper supplier for his *Chicago Examiner* was persuaded to transfer its contract to the *Chicago Herald,* "the only great friendly paper in the middle West," which was in financial difficulties. One of Hearst's agents, H. H. Stansbury, was refused a visa to Great Britain because he worked for Hearst. Even the appointment of a Canadian, F. J. Wilson, to manage the International News Service and Wilson's appeal to the British government through his fellow townsman, the Canadian Tory leader, Arthur Meighan, were not sufficient to soften the attitude of His Majesty's Government; nor did America's entry into the war persuade anyone in London that Hearst would behave.[4]

The president of Columbia University, Dr. Nicholas Murray Butler, advised Sir Gilbert Parker on another aspect of Britain's war propaganda in December 1916. He noted that *The Times, The Spectator* and other major British organs

---

[3] Smith, 77–79.
[4] F.O. 395/70/9285.

"miss almost entirely the salient and outstanding expressions of opinion" in the United States. Better reporting of American affairs was, in Butler's opinion, essential for a good understanding between the two countries.[5] Sir Gilbert was willing to listen.

The formal diplomatic break between the United States and Germany in February 1917 made the propaganda offensive all the more important. The Midwest remained an area of concern for the British government. A traveling British representative, Mr. Walter, informed Lord Eustace Percy in a letter from Kansas City, written on March 30, 1917, of his mission "to arouse pro-Ally sentiment, in which the education of the West seems to be the chief objective." He was cultivating "personal relations" with several hundred local newspaper editors and felt that great progress was being made. The Midwest was far more pro-British than it had been the year before. The only threat to the continuing success of the British effort there was that it would be identified with Wall Street interests: ". . . If these Wall Street people will keep their hands off . . ."[6]

The diplomatic break with Germany aroused great hope that America would soon enter the war on the Allied side. This hope was scarcely dashed by former Secretary of State Bryan's private assurance to the German government that the country was not behind the President. On February 5 the Chief of the Imperial General Staff, Sir William Robertson, wired Colville Barclay, the military attaché in Washington, to find out what sort of an army America would raise if she entered the war. On the same day Spring-Rice cabled to London that, should America become a belligerent, her government would provide the Entente with immediate financial aid.[7]

---

[5] F.O. 395/70/9285.

[6] F.O. 371/3112/7839, 2–4.

[7] F.O. 371/3112/28438/28679.

Barclay's reply to Robertson's enquiry (W.O. 106/467/9379) reached London in two days' time, and the information supplied was realistic. The American Army consisted of about 92,500 men, of which 26,500 men were stationed in various parts of the world. The remainder, about 66,000, were described as good troops. It was estimated that the Army was capable of training about 100,000 fresh recruits at a time. Estimates of the additional contribution which the "Militia" might make were less precise, because exact figures concerning such forces were available only for the Eastern Department. At best the Americans could field about ten divisions "within a year from the date of mobilization."

Robertson was warned that all the troops provided might not be reliable, because there was a large German element in the U.S. which might sabotage American mobilization.

... There are no less than 8½ millions born of German stock and some 2½ millions of these were born in Germany. Among these are a large number of reservists who might give considerable trouble by sabotage of every description. At the outset the danger from this element may be very great, ... At the beginning of the war the Germans had an extensive organization designed to interfere in every possible way with the shipment of munitions etc., to Europe, and clubs were formed all over the country and arms and ammunition were collected. . . . the clubs have been carefully watched and at any moment the arms could be seized. Unfortunately however the police consist largely of German and Irish and it is not known how far they can be trusted. . . .

At best the creation of an American field army would be a "lengthy process," and consequently it was suggested that the American government be encouraged to allow her citizens to volunteer for the Canadian and British armies. The appraisal closed on a pessimistic note.

It is by no means certain that the United States, even if they declared war, would do so with any further object than the protection of their own and other neutral shipping. There appears to be a strong feeling in the United States in favour of limited co-operation for purely American purposes, . . .[8]

During March, Lord Percy worked hard to warn American politicians and officials not to be tricked by German offers of peace. He also painted a grim picture of postwar German commercial competition, which he claimed would be supported by the German government, in order to encourage the Americans to consider continued economic cooperation with Great Britain after the war ended.[9] While Lord Percy beguiled his listeners with tales of the Teutonic economic menace, Colville Barclay advised the Admiralty on how best to secure the cooperation of the United States Navy once America made its decision.[10]

Finally the long-awaited step was taken, and America entered the war. As Spring-Rice reported it, Wilson now saw "that Germany inspired by militariam (sic) is the real enemy,"[11] but he refused to commit the United States to the treaties already signed by the various Allies to regulate the postwar settlement. Despite the good effects of the visit to the United States of the Foreign Secretary, Lord Balfour, America was not always easy to deal with, just as in the years before her entry into the conflict. First there was the danger that in their eagerness to arm the country and take part in the struggle, the United States government would interfere with supplies of raw material and munitions which had been coming to the Allies from American sources. The Foreign Office warned Spring-Rice that he must do everything possible to prevent any disturbance in the regular shipment of supplies.[12] Then there was the question of the expansion of the American Navy. By May the U.S. government had decided upon a program of building capital ships which made the construc-

---

[8] W.O. 106/467/9379.

[9] F.O. 382/15713.

[10] F.O. 371/284387/59547.

[11] F.O. 371/3119/7827.

[12] F.O. 341/3112/7839.

tion of destroyers, viewed by the British as far more important for combating submarines, impossible. Every effort was
called for to make the Americans give up the idea of building
more of these expensive toys. Spring-Rice reported on May
14 that "fear of Japan is so great . . . that we have made no
progress." He suggested that England propose a naval
alliance with the United States to allay such fears.[13]

Four days later, on May 18, the Foreign Office circulated a
memorandum (F.O.371/3119/7827) which concluded that
such an alliance would reflect the realities of the Far Eastern
situation in which "the interests of Great Britain and America
have become increasingly identified." It would serve to check
"Imperialist Japan's" expansion in China as well as any possible threat to the Philippines and could also be expanded to
guard "against unprovoked Japanese aggression against one
of her weaker neighbors such as China, the Dutch East Indies or Siam."

The difficulties which Japan could cause by doing such
things as supporting "the Indian revolutionaries" were also
considered, along with the problem of accurately gauging
Japan's intentions. At the end of this section the following
statement appeared: ". . . we are convinced that in general the
aspirations of Japan are incompatible with the political and
economic necessities of the British Empire. . . . Some risk is
inevitable to ensure our position in the East and Far East
against a danger which we have every reason to believe is a
real one."

To balance such views a postscript was added by another
hand. It argued that the way to end tension between Japan
and America was to persuade America to recognize "Manchuria and Shantung as Japanese spheres of influence in
China, and the ultimate possession by Japan of the islands in
the Pacific north of the Equator. . . ." This could be achieved
by a tripartite naval agreement between Britain, the United

---

[13] F.O. 371/3119/7827.

States, and Japan which would also give the Americans "the
guarantee of the security of the Philippines and Honolulu
against attack." The author of the postscript dismissed the
possibility that Japan and the United States would ever go to
war as "almost unrealisable," because their main military
bases were so far apart.[14] America was already viewed as a
world power with worldwide commitments.

While the Foreign Office was discussing possible naval
alliances, more mundane matters were being considered by
the War Office. America was really quite unprepared for war.
The first step toward helping her to play a role in the actual
fighting in France was to send a military mission under Lieutenant General G. T. M. Bridges to help the Americans in
their efforts. The French dispatched a similar mission under
Marshal Joffre a little later, and the two missions quickly
agreed to follow an "identical policy."

The first British report was not encouraging: "It was found
that the Heads of the Departments at the War Office (i.e.,
War Department) were nearly all too old or too inactive for
the work in hand, especially in the case of the Chief of the
General Staff." General Bridges quickly informed Colonel
Edward House of this fact, and changes were made. The
British would have liked to have seen General Leonard Wood
made Chief of the General Staff, but he was unacceptable to
Wilson because of his close ties with former President Theodore Roosevelt. The mission had to content itself with doing
all they could to encourage the Americans to pass a "Com-
pulsory Service Bill."[15] The general summary of Bridges'
first reports can be found in a General Staff paper dated May
17, 1917: ". . . we cannot expect a considerable U.S.A. Army
to be in the field in any theatre of war for a long time to
come." What amazed the Allied representatives was the total
lack of American preparation. The summary assumed that the

---

[14] F.O. 371/3119/7827.
[15] W.O. 106/468/1-4, 9444.

Americans would be sent over in divisional units and that "linguistic factors will force the Americans to come to us rather than to the French,"[16] i.e., that the Americans would serve with the British. These conclusions paralleled those reached by the intelligence services of the Central Powers.

On June 15, 1917, 10,000 Americans belonging to the First Division left the United States for Saint-Nazaire in France packed aboard 14 troop transports. Bases were being prepared to receive them at Nantes and, for later shipments, at La Pallice, near Bordeaux.[17] The first trickle of what was to become a flood had begun to flow.

The leaders of the Central Powers had spent the preceding year somewhat differently. Statistics had played an ever-increasing role in their thought.

§   Throughout the last part of 1916 German feeling toward the United States had remained suspicious and hostile. This was in part the result of official policy, as the following excerpt from *American Neutrality,* which appeared in the series *Trenchbooks for the German People,* reveals.[18]

We carry carefully framed pictures of the sons of foreign peoples in our head. . . . Originally we had a picture of the Yankee which showed a tobacco chewing, lean, sly dog with a goatee. As an avaricious dollar hunter without any ideals, he lived only for profit, and to earn money he would have sold his soul to the devil and sown radishes on the grave of his parents.

In 1898 we took his picture down from the wall and hung up a new one. To this very day like that of the Englishman it has not

---

[16] W.O. 106/467/9379.

[17] W.O. 106/468/1-4, 9444.

[18] *Flugschriften: Amerika im Weltkreig* 6/2 in the Hauptstaatsarchiv, Stuttgart. Otto von Gottberg, *Amerikanische Neutralitat: Schutzengrabenbücher für das deutsche Volk* (Berlin: Verlag von Karl Siegismund, 1916).

dried, because it rains virtues. We admired the Americans as "people of the future" in the "land of unlimited possibilities" until we felt the devilish effect of American shells. . . . Nevertheless few Germans expected from the United States such an unfriendly neutrality as we are now experiencing. In order to investigate its cause we must view the American people from the hour of their birth through German eyes. . . . the Americans are Anglo-Saxons and if not by blood, still in spirit pure Englishmen! . . . . (3–5)

.   .   .   .   .

It would be a miracle if a people with a history which tells only of the desire for profit would not also simply pursue profit in the most terrible bloodletting of all time. Under the guise of maintaining a supposed neutrality which is hostile to us, the Americans supply Germany's enemies with all the resources of war. They desire to enrich themselves and also seek our defeat. . . . The collapse of the British Empire would cause the ruling alliance between capital and politics in the United States a greater financial loss than the destruction of the German Empire, because more American capital is invested in English than in German businesses. Further the Americans fear neither the economic, nor the political, nor the military power of Britain. . . . On the other hand they view with mistrustful, hostile respect the cleverness, diligence, and success of the German businessman, technician, soldier, or seaman. . . .

Therefore the Americans are our enemies. . . . (43–44)

.   .   .   .   .

The economic intervention of America in the war could be more significant than the military. The United States was and is our economic opponent. Whether or not they maintain neutrality, they will be our strongest trade competitors after this war which has been so exhausting for Europe. They are already seeking to win the former German markets in China, South America and especially in the portion of Europe hostile to us. The success of their plans would reduce the profit of the German merchant and worker. The Americans protected from the war, and indeed enriched by it, will at first be better equipped than we to compete when peace comes and if we do not gather all our national strength and employ it in the further development of our economy they will bring to bear an almost crushing commercial superiority. . . . (47)

PA XXXIII 52 folio 197
Chargé Zwiedenek to Baron Burián

8 June 1916

[Zwiedenek reported a speech made by Secretary Lansing about foreign policy. Lansing had answered the charge that he was more intransigent with Germany. Zwiedenek interpreted the speech as a campaign speech.] The different standard by which the present administration judges both power blocs was too obvious to be disposed of so simply with the slogan that there is a difference between life and mere property. The administration have not merely observed a corresponding gradation in the harshness of the means employed in response to the English violation of the law but in fact have done nothing except write notes which contained no serious threat. On the other hand they have defended stubbornly against Germany such rights as those of a nation at war to arm merchant ships without the loss of their character as peaceful vessels which, according to the doctrine of (international law) itself, is doubtful.

The attitude expressed in the note concerning the natural and obligatory restraint of responsible statesmen with the warlike gestures of irresponsible private critics sounds false after the administration have at various times by their formally provocative attitude placed the United States in danger of being drawn into the World War not so much to maintain vital rights but rather for political reasons. . . .

§   The hope of victory was still strong. A few days after the beginning of the Somme offensive von Nagel wrote to the Bavarian War Minister.

M. Kr. 1830
Von Nagel to Minister of War

No. 7880   GHQSM   8.7.16

[Speaking generally of the war] If this great general offensive of

the Entente does not defeat us, then France and probably also
Russia could become so discouraged that peace will be brought
nearer even against England's will.

§   The attitude toward submarine warfare began to change.

M. Kr. 1830

Major von Pappus[19] to the Bavarian Minister of War

No. 8001   GHQSM   11.8.16

. . . I have heard but without confirmation, that negotiations concerning the intensification of the submarine war have resulted in no
agreement. . . .

Two weeks later Falkenhayn's dismissal and the appointment of Hindenburg and Ludendorff to the positions of high
command were reported.[20] The war had reached a turning
point and the question of unrestricted submarine warfare was
an ever more pressing issue.

In a later report on submarine warfare, the Bavarian military plenipotentiary at Berlin, von Köppel, again reported the
Chancellor's words to the Reichstag on September 29, 1916.

M. Kr. 41

No. 8186   GHQSM   29.9.16

. . . The Chancellor referred to his statements in March and May

---

[19] Major Freiherr Eckhart von Pappus und Tratzberg served as the deputy
to the various Bavarian military plenipotentiaries at Supreme Headquarters
until the end of the war. He was a particularly acute observer and shared
with General Paul Ritter von Köberle, the last plenipotentiary, a realistic and
critical attitude toward the policies and strategy of Hindenburg and Ludendorff.

[20] M. Kr. 1831, No. 8392, 29.8.16.

of this year concerning submarine warfare and emphasized that the question of unrestricted submarine warfare must be decided entirely from a technical point of view, even if it will result in a break with America, but that the decision whether or not to employ it remains a question of the conduct of the war. [He then called upon Admiral von Capelle, who guaranteed that 600,000 tons of enemy shipping a month could be sunk] . . . "if unrestricted submarine warfare against all enemy and neutral ships carrying contraband goods were to be waged. . . ."

PA XXXIII 52 folio 338, 339, 336

Chargé Zwiedenek to Burián

WASHINGTON, 15 November, 1916

[Zwiedenek reported on the Republican defeat. He blamed Theodore Roosevelt for not doing more to help Chief Justice Hughes.] But still the attitude towards foreign policy certainly played a much greater role this time than was the case in previous elections and the decision in favor of Wilson probably resulted from the hope that under his administration the country would continue to keep out of the war. It is ironic for Wilson that those States of the Union which have profited most from America's friendly attitude towards the Allies and in which pro-Allied elements were also much more predominant voted against him. The small gratitude for his pro-British attitude which Wilson has experienced during the campaign, and the desire, which was especially clearly manifested in certain states, to remain at peace, should logically influence favorably the President's behavior and offers a certain consolation for those who had awaited from a Hughes administration an improvement of relations with the Central Powers. . . .

. . . However the fact cannot be ignored that at least for a while Wilson was not disinclined to join the Allies and that the danger of a break with America could again suddenly become a grave threat. . . . Because no one can be sure what would be the effect of America's entry into the World War—and it could possibly mean a catastrophe—it is hardly enough to urge submarine commanders to exercise the greatest caution. The means are sufficient even when the dose is increased more slowly and a few less ships are torpedoed.

German Foreign Ministry 21/380

Mr. Warburg to State Secretary Dr. Zimmermann

HAMBURG, 18th December, 1916

[Mr. Warburg reported that the Federal Reserve Board had forbidden the acceptance of any further short-term loans from the Entente.] The Americans are finally saturated with Allied bonds and as long as some especially inept behavior on our part does not again stimulate it, no new enthusiasm for Allied bonds will reappear. A confidant has confirmed my impression that they intend to send Colonel House to Europe again in the near future.

§   The German Navy was busy preparing its arguments for unlimited submarine warfare.

PK VIII ¹/₁₉ Kriegsarchiv, Vienna

B 35 840 I   BERLIN, 22 December, 1916

The Chief of the Admiralty Staff of the Navy to
the Royal Field Marshal,
Chief of the General Staff of the Fieldarmy,
Mr. von Beneckendorff and von Hindenburg, Excellency

Top Secret!

Your Excellency, I have the honor to submit most respectfully in the enclosed a report concerning the necessity for the early commencement of unrestricted submarine warfare. The paper is essentially a continuation of the memorandum "The Tonnage Question and the Provision of England in the Year 1916," which was also sent to Your Excellency with the designation No. 22,247 I of the 27th of August 1916.

May I beg Your Excellency to listen to the following argument which is based upon a thorough study of the enclosed? I hope we can entirely agree that it is absolutely necessary to intensify to the utmost our campaign against England's seaborne traffic as soon as possible, in order to ensure ourselves a quick victory.

I.

If the war is not to end in the general exhaustion of all sides which would be fateful for us, it must be decided before the fall of 1917. Among our enemies the economies of Italy and France are so weakened that they are only maintained by England's energy and achievements. If we should succeed in breaking England's backbone, the war would quickly be decided in our favor. But England's backbone is the shipping which brings to the British Isles the supplies necessary to maintain life, to support war industry and to ensure solvency to other countries.

II.

The present state of the ship tonnage question, which was thoroughly discussed in the paper of the 27th of August, is once again described in the enclosed. In brief it is the following:

Cargoes in a great number of vital areas have increased immensely, sometimes tenfold or more. We know for sure from numerous other sources that there is a universal shortage of shipping space.

At present English tonnage can be accurately estimated at about 20 million gross registered tons. [B.R.T.]. Of these at least 8.6 million tons are employed in coastal shipping. It is estimated that roughly one million tons are being repaired or else are unused. Approximately 2 million tons must be employed to serve the Allies, so that there are only 8 million tons available to supply England. A statistical study of seaborne traffic using English ports shows that the amount is even less: during the months of July–September 1916, only about $6\frac{3}{4}$ million B.R.T. were available. Besides this, it can be estimated that 900,000 tons of enemy shipping–not of English origin–sail to England along with a good 3 million tons of neutral shipping. All in all, England is being supplied with only about $10\frac{3}{4}$ million B.R.T.

III.

If further action along the lines of the work which has already been accomplished in the struggle against enemy shipping appears to be promising, then the unusually bad yield of the world's crop of cereal grains and fodder has presented us with a really splendid opportunity of which it would be criminal not to take advantage. North America and Canada will probably not be able to supply

England with grain beyond February. After that she must draw her supplies by the long route from Argentina, but since as a result of its bad harvest, Argentina can only supply little, grain must come from India and primarily from Australia. The enclosed explains in detail that such a lengthening of the import route compels our enemy to employ an additional 720,000 tons for the transport of grain. This means that up to August 1917 three quarters of a million tons of the available $10^{3}\!/_{4}$ million tons will be required for a task which was until now not at all necessary.

IV.

Under such favorable conditions an energetic blow delivered with full force against English shipping promises such sure success, that I can only repeat and emphasize my statement of the 27th of August 1916, "Therefore our obvious war aim is to achieve a decision in our favor now by the destruction of shipping space" and further "from a military standpoint it is irresponsible to make no use of the U-boat weapon now." I do not hesitate to say that, in view of the present situation, we could force England to peace within five months by means of unrestricted submarine warfare. This applies however only to unrestricted submarine warfare; it does not apply to the submarine cruiser warfare which is currently being carried on, not even if all armed ships could be fired upon.

· · ·

VI.

The proclamation of unrestricted submarine warfare will once again pose for the United States of America the question of whether or not she wishes to accept the consequences of the attitude which she has previously taken. I am fully convinced that war with America is such a serious matter that everything should be done in order to avoid it. But in my opinion the reluctance to face a break should not cause us to be afraid to use at the decisive moment a weapon which promises us victory.

In any case it is best to assume that America's decision is more likely to be unfavorable to us and to be clear about what influence America's joining our enemies would have upon the course of the war. This influence could only be very limited with respect to ship tonnage. No more than a small fraction of the tonnage of the Central Powers lying in American and perhaps in other neutral harbors could be employed immediately in the journey to England. The far greater part will be so damaged that in the decisive period of the first months they would not be able to sail. The preparations for this have already been made. In addition there would be no crew available for the ships. American troops could be expected to have an equally small decisive effect, because of the shipping shortage. They could not be brought over in large numbers and American money could not replace the missing supplies and ships. The only question which remains is how would America act when England is forced to conclude peace. There is no reason to assume that she would then decide to continue the war alone against us, for she would have no means available to move against us decisively, while her seaborne traffic would be damaged by our U-boats. Indeed she can be expected to join the English in the conclusion of peace in order to restore her economy to normalcy as quickly as possible.

Therefore I conclude that unrestricted submarine warfare, begun at the proper time, so that it leads to peace before the world harvest of the summer of 1917, that is before the 1st of August, is worth even the risk of a break with America, because no other choice remains for us. In spite of the danger of a break with America, an early start to unrestricted submarine warfare is the proper means to end the war victoriously. It is also the only way to achieve this end.

VII.

. . . If we fail to take advantage of this chance, which as far as can be judged, is the last chance, then I see no other result than mutual exhaustion without our being able to end the war in such a way that our future as a world power will be assured.

In order to achieve the necessary effect at the proper time, unrestricted U-boat warfare must begin at the latest on February 1. I beg Your Excellency to say whether the military situation on the Continent, especially with respect to the remaining neutral nations, will allow us to begin at this time. I need a period of three weeks to undertake the necessary preparations.

(Signed) v. HOLTZENDORFF

§   The Bavarian plenipotentiary reported to his government on December 29 as follows:

M. Kr. 1830

No. 9410   GHQSM   29.12.16

Today a discussion took place between the Imperial Chancellor and Hindenburg and Ludendorff; tomorrow Zimmermann is expected here. I have not yet been able to find out if it concerned a decision about submarine warfare, or the arrival of the Entente's reply to the peace note, but today's conference has been described to me as a very "critical day."

§   Two days later the truth was known. Von Pappus reported:

M. Kr. 1830

No. 9431   GHQSM   31.12.16

The conversations of the Supreme Command with the Imperial Chancellor and Zimmermann have reestablished a good understanding between the civil and military authorities. His Majesty, the Emperor, has agreed to a so-called intensified U-boat warfare, but not to a completely unrestricted campaign, as was actually desired. Nevertheless a not inconsiderable increase in enemy shipping losses and forfeiture of tonnage is expected from the intensified form.

§   The new year brought a further report delivered by von Pappus.

M. Kr. 1831

No. 9461   GHQSM   3.1.17

The government wishes to await the official delivery of the Entente's reply before beginning the so-called intensified form submarine warfare and then it is to be carried on in the same way it was in May of last year, when, on account of America, this kind of U-boat warfare was suspended. The aim is to sink armed merchant ships without warning. The Navy doesn't expect a significant increase compared with the successes achieved so far but believes it will be possible to maintain the level which has already been reached. The right time to wage relentless submarine warfare will come when the military have taken the proper measures to meet possible intervention on the part of Holland and Denmark. This will only be possible after the close of the Rumanian offensive, which has at present been somewhat delayed. But once the necessary troops are available and in position, then the question of unrestricted submarine warfare will again become acute and call for a decision which might well present an "either or choice" between the Chancellor and Hindenburg.

§   The German government moved closer to a decision. Von Pappus again reported:

M. Kr. 1831

No. 9501   GHQSM   7.1.17

... This morning Admiral von Holtzendorff arrived for a conference with Excellency Ludendorff. The question of submarine warfare is to be more carefully considered.

§   And two days later:

M. Kr. 1831

No. 9511   GHQSM   9.1.17

... The Imperial Chancellor arrived today. Important decisions about the U-boat war are to be made. Admiral von Holtzendorff is still here. ...

§   The next day the Admiral and the Chancellor left GHQ
and two days after that, on January 12, von Pappus reported:

M. Kr. 1831

No. 9531   GHQSM   12.1.17

Precautionary measures against Holland and Denmark are being
prepared.[In case of war Holland was to be attacked from Belgium
and Germany. Little resistance was expected from Denmark.] The
attitude of the Japanese Foreign Minister is said to be very reserved
and should America intervene against us, a change (in the Japanese
attitude) is possible, because such a decision would provide Japan
with an excellent opportunity to move against an already occupied
America. In this case Japan would require a guarantee that she
would not be attacked from the rear from Russia, and this might well
influence her in our favor. The Foreign Office is more sceptical of
such an optimistic view of these possibilities. They do not believe
that a more energetic submarine campaign will cause the automatic
suspension of relations with America, but rather that America will at
first exercise caution and observe the effects of this measure and
then act only if we violate the intended agreement. The Navy does
not believe that Holland and Sweden will intervene. . . .

§   Five days later von Pappus narrated the progress of the
discussions. He began with an explanation of Admiral von
Holtzendorff's opinion.

M. Kr. 1831

No. 9589   GHQSM   17.1.17

Excellency von Holtzendorff argues that it is absolutely necessary
to increase to the utmost our campaign against England's sea traffic
as soon as possible, in order to exploit the advantage of the present
situation and to secure for ourselves a speedy victory. . . .

§   On the same day von Pappus reported:

M. Kr. 1831

No. 9581   GHQSM   17.1.17

The German ambassador [in Washington], Count Bernstorff, is now said to be in complete agreement with unrestricted submarine warfare. I have not been able to discover the reasons which caused him to change his mind. . . .

§   And then three days later:

M. Kr. 1831

No. 9621   GHQSM   20.1.17

Today unrestricted submarine warfare [in the war zone] begins against merchant ships. Our note has been delivered to America but she has not yet responded to it. It is believed that for the moment she will do nothing. . . .

§   Von Pappus told his superiors that the American reply caused no great concern at G.H.Q.

M. Kr. 1831

No. 9671   GHQSM   25.1.17

Wilson's note is not taken seriously here . . . . America's intervention on the side of the Entente is considered almost certain. But for the moment nothing can be said (for sure), because there are also reports which claim that North American popular opinion has changed significantly in favor of Germany.

§   Two days later von Pappus sent another report to the Bavarian War Minister.

M. Kr. 1831

No. 9690   GHQSM   27.1.17

. . . Submarine warfare without any restriction begins on the 1st of February; on 2.2 it also begins against hospital ships, which obviously have ammunition and troops on board. . . .

§   Von Pappus announced the arrival of Zimmermann.

M. Kr. 1831

No. 9731   GHQSM   31.1.17

[He had arrived on the 29th and had sought to delay the start of the submarine campaign until Wilson's note arrived. Bernstorff had reported that the note offered new opportunities for peace negotiations. Zimmermann's efforts failed and the scheduled resumption of restricted submarine warfare took place on February 1. Von Pappus noted that the Germans had made concessions to the Americans. American ships traveling under their own flag were to be allowed to pass through certain specific areas of the war zone. The report continued with a reflection of optimism. The Navy had enough submarines to maintain the effort against England's supply lines and any U-boat losses could be made good from new construction.] In contrast to the opinions expressed in diplomatic circles, which believe war with America is unlikely, in Navy circles war with America is viewed as certain. There will be no lack of efforts to bring about a return to restricted submarine warfare as soon as complications with America occur, and these may be taken as certain. The OHL is completely determined to continue to employ the measures which have now been taken. . . .

§   Efforts at least to delay the reintroduction of unrestricted submarine warfare were not long in coming. Von Pappus's report explained that the Chancellor and his advisers wanted to send a last-minute message to the United States announcing a delay in the resumption of the U-boat war. General von Plessen, however, intervened with the Emperor, and Bethmann's wishes were thwarted. Von Pappus added that there was a growing desire among some to see Bethmann replaced by Tirpitz.[21]

Von Köppel reported the Chancellor's speech from Berlin.

M. Kr. 41

No. 1221   GHQSM   31.1.1917

[The peace offer had been rejected because the enemy's sole desire was to dictate peace. It was therefore now necessary to win the war, and consequently the issue of U-boat warfare was a vital question. Earlier it had been irresponsible to employ this method but now it was necessary. Germany had a greater number of submarines and due to the smallness of the world's grain harvest, they could be employed to influence the enemy and hopefully to cause England's allies to desert her. The Chancellor expressed his doubt that unrestricted submarine warfare would affect neutrals.] And America? Obviously we are doing everything to keep America out of the war. I do not know if we shall be successful. America remains an uncertain factor in our calculations; I know what America's participation in the war would mean, therefore I take the matter very seriously, not merely on account of the war itself but also in terms of the peace which will follow. Still American intervention no longer represents the danger it formerly did, for (1) her entry will no longer have the effect upon the European neutrals it once would have had, and (2) the conditions in all the countries waging war point to an end [of the conflict] which can be expected before America's influence will be felt.

---

[21] M. Kr. 1831, No. 9740, 1.2.17.

If unrestricted submarine warfare has the desired effect, then America does not have the time necessary [to make her influence felt]; it is no longer the "silver bullet" which is decisive, but rather the "bronze cannon" [von Köppel then reported what Hindenburg had said to him.] Hindenburg said to me, "the Front holds firm, morale is good, the men are confident and if the Hindenburg Program is carried out, success can be expected. We can accept the disadvantages, which submarine warfare may cause us because England will be forced to (make) peace. Our allies agree with us; Austria has shown her support by declaring a restricted zone around Italy. . . ."

§   Events moved swiftly. Von Pappus reported to the Minister of War about the diplomatic break with America.

M. Kr. 1831

No. 9771   GHQSM   5.2.17

. . . The break in relations with America came sooner than it was expected here, but an imminent declaration of war is not awaited, and some go as far as to describe the break as only a bluff, made in order to persuade us to suspend unrestricted submarine warfare, which we do not intend to do. On the other hand the Navy believes that America will soon declare war. It is thought possible that Japan will make use of this opportunity to gain Hongkong and Tonking for herself, once America is fully involved with us.

§   The Emperor's view of Wilson's reaction was of importance to the Bavarian government. Von Pappus seems to have reported the All Highest's view of Wilson's action with a certain subtle pleasure.

M. Kr. 1831

No. 9801   GHQSM   8.2.17

His Majesty is very satisfied with the attitude of the neutrals. With respect to Wilson's dissimilar handling of the German and Austrian ambassadors, His Majesty thinks that America would like to drive a wedge between us and Austria and cause disunity. His Majesty also said that Wilson did not want to quarrel with the ancient dynasty of the Habsburgs, but viewed the Hohenzollerns as mere parvenues and who had done all the damage!

§ The military had won a great domestic victory at the beginning of February, but that victory had its price, as General von Hartz's memorandum to Munich demonstrates. General von Hartz had replaced von Nagel at GHQSM.

M. Kr. 1831

No. 9987   GHQSM   28.2.17

Thank God that the public believes there is unity and cordial cooperation between the General Staff and the civilian who directs imperial policy (Bethmann), but this is in fact not the case. Everyone here is rather strongly opposed to the Imperial Chancellor and would very much like to see him replaced. The far reaching war aims which Dr. Wildgrube's recent statements in the Prussian Landtag, and at the meeting of the League of German Farmers expressed are sympathized with here. Naval representatives here take particular delight in Mr. von Bethmann's supposed fear of the impetuous deeds performed by our submarines against neutral ships.

The language of the General Staff with the Foreign Office has always been quite clear. The use of this tone toward the so-called "spineless ones" is considered absolutely necessary. [Von Hartz was critical of army influence; he said the Chancellor had given in but that, as a result, things had not gone well politically.]

§ The implementation of the decision to resume unrestricted submarine warfare seemed to bear fruit. General von Hartz sent home the following figures to the Bavarian Minister of War.

M. Kr. 1831

No. 10201   GHQSM   17.3.17

U-boat sinkings in February: 781,000 tons, which included 644,000 tons of enemy and 137,000 tons of neutral shipping. The result exceeds the expectations of the Navy.

§ Even after America's decision to wage war upon the side of the Entente, no one in Berlin gave the impression of being unduly concerned, for the statistics presented by the Navy were so very convincing. This was not the case in Vienna. Baron Burián's successor as Foreign Minister, Ottokar Graf (Count) Czernin von und zu Chudenitz, was frankly worried. As the two following reports reveal, the Germans found a number of Austrians willing to attempt to reassure him. On May 1 the Austrian ambassador in Bern had his say and on May 2 the Austrian naval adviser at Austrian Supreme Headquarters reported to his superior in Vienna the results of a visit to the Headquarters by the Chief of the German Naval Staff.

OK 2533, Kriegsarchiv, Vienna

Baron Musulin to Count Czernin

The efficacy of German Submarine Warfare.

No. 65/P.-B.   BERN, 1 May, 1917

It is well known that the skepticism with which we in

Austria-Hungary viewed the effect of submarine warfare, particularly unrestricted submarine warfare, has been shared by many German diplomats and politicians. Here in Switzerland where I have had the opportunity to discuss the problems of submarine warfare with German diplomats and German notables who were passing through, I have encountered much shaking of heads and many misgivings. The general opinion was usually that submarine warfare caused some unpleasantness and inconvenience for our enemies but did not really represent a serious threat to them. It was pointed out that the Central Powers were also subjected to a hunger blockade and did not succumb to it. . . . Doubts about the effectiveness of the U-boats were increased by the Entente's excellent press campaign. . . .

Only about three weeks ago did I first find in the French papers clear signs of a critical situation in vital areas of production which was the direct result of submarine warfare. As yet a frank and open admission cannot be found in the French press, but in the treatment of technical and commercial questions, admissions which the censor has obviously overlooked or wanted to overlook, leave as far as clarity is concerned little to be desired. I refer to: the crisis in the French oil industry which elicited the cry, "no more ships arrive!" from the author of the short paragraph about it; the complete lack of tin plate which threatens the food supply of Sarrail's army;[22] the impossibility of replacing tin cans for the production of canned food with the products of the glass industry which itself suffers from a shortage of all necessities; the official control of the flour supply which even affects religious life, etc., etc.

English press reports which in recent weeks have been remarkably frank have revealed clearly that England also has great problems with her food supply. This has obviously been done because the English wished to show the French that they did not suffer alone. . . .

In the German Embassy here the former critics of the U-boat campaign have become silent. There has been greater optimism since the arrival of news that the food crisis in Germany has become less acute. It is expected that with improved weather and longer days — in short with the coming of the high season for U-boats — even

---

[22] In Greece.

greater numerical successes can be recorded and we will be brought closer to peace.

PK VIII ¹/₁₉ Kriegsarchiv, Vienna

Imperial and Royal Army Supreme Command Naval Adviser

Secret

May 2, 1917

Your Excellency!

I hasten to inform you about the outcome of today's visit by His Excellency the Chief of the German Naval Staff.

Originally, the visit in Baden was planned merely to introduce Admiral von Holtzendorff to the new Chief of the General Staff. However, the German plenipotentiary, General von Cramon, arranged for His Majesty to receive the German Admiral in an audience and then to command him with his whole suite and my humble self to join him at breakfast.

The purpose of the audience was to eliminate by means of a direct report the influence of Count Czernin, who still doubts the real success of submarine warfare. This seems to have been accomplished in the course of the unusually long audience — circa fifty minutes — and during and after the breakfast both Majesties revealed[23] a quite extraordinary good humor. In any case the Imperial reception was remarkably gracious.

Afterwards Admiral von Holtzendorff had a long discussion with His Excellency Freiherr von Arz,[24] in which, as far as I know, complete agreement on the issue of submarine warfare was reached. . . .

.   .   .   .   .

Allow me, Your Excellency, the expression of my most obedient respect wherewith I remain Your Excellency's most humble (servant),

WINTERHALTER, *Rear-Admiral*

---

[23] The Emperor and Empress.
[24] The Austrian Chief of staff.

§   Not everyone was delighted by the turn of events, especially after the American declaration of war in April. Von
Pappus reported the views of Mr. von Krupp-Bohlen.

M. Kr. 1831

No. 1130   GHQSM   31.5.17

... All sides long for the end of the war but it is not yet in sight,
because the Entente have done everything to prolong the war as long
as possible so that we will feel the impact of American intervention. ...

§   The significance of the American entry into the war was
not merely confined to its impact upon the Central Powers.
The British were concerned about the U.S. role as a Pacific
power. They considered a naval alliance with the United
States both to dissuade her from building capital ships rather
than destroyers and to meet the needs of their own postwar
policy in the Pacific.

F.O. 371/3119/7827

FOREIGN OFFICE, May 18th, 1917

I circulate the annexed Foreign Office Minutes. The subject is of
the greatest urgency and importance
(*Initialled*)   R.C. (ROBERT CECIL)

Sir C. Spring-Rice's telegram, May 14th 1917 (annexed)

PROPOSED NAVAL ALLIANCE WITH THE UNITED STATES

The Far Eastern Department have examined the question under
the following headings: —

1. Is it contrary to (a) the letter or (b) the spirit of the Anglo-Japanese Alliance?

2. Would it necessarily antagonise Japan to the extent of virtually abrogating the Anglo-Japanese Alliance?

3. In this case, in what political direction could or would Japan seek to damage us in return?

4. Is it necessary or expedient to communicate it to the Japanese Government?

1. The intention of Article 4 of the Treaty of Alliance between Great Britain and Japan was expressly to exclude America from its scope. This may reasonably be held to have become operative by the conclusion of the Anglo-American Treaty (although not strictly an Arbitration Treaty) of September 15th, 1914. Consequently an Anglo-American Alliance would not be contrary to the strict letter of the Anglo-Japanese Alliance.

On the other hand, although the Anglo-Japanese Alliance was concluded in respect of a political sphere in which America was held, for purposes of the Treaty, to be disinterested, she is in effect an important factor in that sphere and is potentially the main Far Eastern antagonist of our Japanese Ally. An Alliance between Great Britain and the United States is therefore bound to qualify the solidarity and effectiveness of the Anglo-Japanese Alliance — all the more, as, since its conclusion, the Far Eastern interests of Great Britain and America have become increasingly identified and those of Great Britain and Japan have become correspondingly estranged. The new proposal would set a formal seal on this new orientation of British policy and would to that extent be contrary to the spirit of the Anglo-Japanese Alliance. . . .

B. Imperialist Japan's future lies in China and the Pacific. Already American intervention in the war has ipso facto modified the international situation in the Far East and has imposed an effective check on Japanese aspirations. An Alliance of any kind between Great Britain and America involves a formal rapproachement between the two countries with incalculable potentialities to the detriment of a Japanese forward policy. America admittedly desires the role of protector of China against Japanese aggression, in itself a defensive policy, and, if we formally ally ourselves with her, we potentially abet her in carrying it out. Consequently the defensive Naval Alliance with America deals in reality the most decisive blow at what has become Japan's traditional policy in the Far East, namely Japanese penetration of China in the Pacific (involving incidentally a menace to the Philippines) under the protection of the Anglo-Japanese Alliance.

In any case it is clear that, the suggested Anglo-American Alliance, would involve combination of the two countries against a Japanese attack on America or on the British colonies. But further there cannot fail to be strong presumption in favour of any form of alliance with America, however "defensive" in name, in practice gradually expanding into an arrangement of wider scope, and involving a combination for instance against unprovoked Japanese aggression against one of her weaker neighbours such as China, the Dutch East Indies or Siam.

However this may be, Japan can hardly fail to regard any blunt announcement of an alliance of any kind between us and America as sounding the death knell of her more predatory ambitions and, even if the Japanese Government considered that present conditions demanded acquiescence explosion of public opinion is almost inevitable.

3. It is certain that, in adhering to the Anglo-Japanese Alliance, Japan is prompted by pure self-interest and not by considerations of ideal loyalty. There is strong circumstantial proof that she has not severed all connexion with Germany. Only the naval and military authorities can say how far we should be damaged by her throwing her naval and military strength on the other side now. It is however obvious that her position is ultimately threatened by the growth of the naval and military forces of America. She can do now what she will not be able to do two years hence.

Considered politically, she could either declare openly against the Allies and combine with Mexico against the United States, or, more subtly, could "resort to pressure" against Russia, to use the words of the Japanese Minister for Foreign Affairs, by an attack on Russian Manchuria or she could give open support to the Indian revolutionaries, or again, less sensationally, she could create chaos in China for purposes of intervention or abet a Manchu restoration under her aegis and so provoke a Far Eastern crisis which would enable her in a German-Japanese interest to divert attention from the war and seriously embarrass us. A less drastic, but still inconvenient, revenge would be her withdrawal on some pretext of the destroyers which she has sent to the Mediterranean and the other warships which she has sent elsewhere.

4. A secret treaty between America and ourselves appears to be

impossible under the American constitution but in any case it would be undoubtedly inconsistent with the spirit of the Anglo-Japanese Alliance that we shall withhold from Japan the conclusion of a naval alliance with America. The real reason would no doubt be pointed out to her and we should add that we were so convinced of her pacific intentions towards America that we had no hesitation in accepting the American condition in full confidence that she would understand the position. The Japanese Government might thereupon find no formal ground on which to protest, but its publication in Japan could hardly fail to create a huge sensation and the very considerable violent elements in the country that are already op-posed to the Anglo-Japanese Alliance would not improbably cause the fall of the present insecure Government if it accepted it without a murmur.

The above propositions are founded only on such conclusions as to Japanese intentions as can be drawn from the necessarily limited information at our disposal, Japan being of all countries the most difficult to fathom politically, and involve an element of conjecture and prophecy which is clearly an unsafe guide. But from a study of contemporary events in the Far East during the last five and partic-ularly the last two years, we are convinced that in general the aspirations of Japan are incompatible with the political and economic necessities of the British Empire and that the Anglo-Japanese Al-liance of 1911 no longer forms a working basis for relations between the two countries and therefore already reposes on a very flimsy basis. If this assumption is pressed to its logical conclusion and no other practical working basis can be found then either one side or the other must forego its aspirations or we must come to blows. The formal rapprochement with America, now proposed can be in-terpreted in no other way but as having a direct bearing on the situation in the Far East and can therefore hardly fail to constitute the first rift in Anglo-Japanese relations.

Such are the possibilities of danger to which we feel bound to call attention. The broad political and strategic advantages of the new proposal are on the other hand from our point of view incalculable. The Alliance with America would safeguard our Imperial interests from Wei Hai Wei to Australia and back to Singapore, Colombo and Suez, while, should it mature into a formal "Entente" for purposes of our joint Chinese policy, we shall have laid the foundations of a future entirely favourable to our own political and commercial interests. Some risk is inevitable to ensure the future of our position in the East and Far East against a danger which we have every reason to believe is a real one.

(Initialled)   J.D.G.

On the other hand there can be little doubt that the Americans and Japanese are mutually suspicious of each other. The Americans fear an attack by Japan on the Philippines, Honolulu and even the American continent. The Japanese are suspicious of the attitude of the United States in their attempts to thwart Japanese aspirations in China. There is no reason to believe that Japan harbours any intention of attacking America and it would be to the advantage of both countries to have such suspicions removed. So also a frank recognition by the United States Government of Manchuria and Shantung as Japanese spheres of influence in China, and the ultimate possession by Japan of the islands in the Pacific north of the equator, should go far to remove any suspicion of American hostility towards moderate Japanese ambitions. Further the immense intervening distances between the principal military and naval bases of both countries render a conflict almost unrealisable. Consequently some form of mutual insurance of both the United States and Japan would be desirable in the interests of both countries, and it is not impossible that this might be effected to the advantage of all concerned by the conclusion of a tri-partite defensive alliance between Great Britain, the United States and Japan. The advantage to be derived by Japan from such an alliance would be the recognition by the United States of a Japanese sphere of influence in China. The United States would profit by the guarantee of the security of the Philippines and Honolulu against attack; while both Japan and the United States would gain by the removal of prevailing suspicion between them. The advantages of such a policy to Great Britain are obvious. It might be difficult to find a formula to meet the conflicting interests of the United States and Japan in China and to remove existing suspicion between the two Powers, but this should not be beyond the skill of diplomacy to devise. It must be remembered, however, that this is a question which should not be dealt with precipitately and which will require delicate handling, otherwise we run the risk of driving the Japanese into the enemy's camp.

(Initialled)   H. of P.

CHAPTER IV

The Grand Tour Begins

§   While Wilson talked of a peace which would grant the world justice and freedom, and in August 1917 Pope Benedict XV appealed to the warring nations for such a peace, the war went on. The Allies were too busy with the practical problems of maintaining their war effort to pay that much attention to Wilson's ideological formulations. The Bolshevik Revolution (October 1917) took Russia out of the war, and Italy almost suffered a similar fate after the disaster at Caporetto, which also occurred at the end of October 1917. In addition, until the very last months of the year, the German submarine offensive achieved even more than those who had supported unrestricted submarine warfare had promised. The convoy was finally adopted to combat the submarine and, in combination with new detection devices, managed by the end of 1917 to confine British losses within acceptable limits.[1] The Allied problem was complicated by the difficulties which had overtaken the French.

General Robert Nivelle's April offensive along the Chemin des Dames ridge, which he had claimed held the key to victory, was a fiasco. The German retreat to the Siegfried (Hindenburg) line had already taken place before the assault.

---

[1] C. R. M. F. Cruttwell, *A History of the Great War, 1914–1918* (Oxford: Clarendon Press, 1934), 384–385.

97

The Germans had every advantage. Their defenses were carefully prepared; they were able to employ their new tactics of defense in depth and they knew of Nivelle's plans in advance. The bloody failure was too much for the French infantry.[2] Antiwar agitation had already begun before the attack. The skillfully prepared propaganda of certain agitators fell upon fertile soil. The leave policy of the French Army was poor, the relations between officers and men stiff and very distant, and the medical provision for the wounded fell far below the standard of either the British or the German Army. Worst of all, there was the contrast between the fate of those in the trenches and the sweet life and high pay of those who had been excused from military service to work in France's vital war industries. More than 50 divisions were affected by the mutiny, and it took all of Pétain's skill to restore discipline to the French Army.

It was up to Haig and his armies to bear the brunt of the fighting. The British offensive that aimed at taking the Wytschaete-Messines ridge as the first step towards regaining the Belgian coast and, among other things, closing down the German submarine bases there had been delayed to accommodate Neville. Despite the initial success at Messines, in June, before the opening of the battle itself, rain, mud, and the German defense in depth (elastic defense) prevented the British from doing much except suffer heavy losses. Though probably not as costly as the Somme, Third Ypres (or Passchendaele, as it is remembered) left an indelible impression upon the minds of those who took part in it, as well as those who later wrote the history of the war. Like the Somme, Passchendaele imposed very heavy losses upon the Germans as well and certainly contributed to the continuing deterioration of the German Army.[3] At that time most people thought

---

[2] Cruttwell, 400–404, 411–413.
[3] Cruttwell, 440–443.

of a successful war in terms of the destruction of the enemy's army. Third Ypres did contribute to this process.

Certain aspects of Haig's attitude toward the battle are of interest here. In June he argued that the attack that began at the end of July was necessary to encourage the French, because the prospect of American help was too remote to keep up French morale. At the end of October he opposed abandoning the offensive because it meant giving up the initiative until 1919, when the Americans would be strong enough to regain it.[4] The result was that by the end of November he did not have sufficient reserves to exploit the remarkably successful attack launched at Cambrai on November 20 under the cover of large masses of tanks. Before the battle was over, the British suffered a sharp reverse because they lacked the men necessary to consolidate their initial gains.[5]

The fact that the British failed to exploit the Cambrai breakthrough contributed to the German conclusion that they need not be unduly concerned about the tanks. The German counterattack also revealed a German weakness. At the high point of their success, one German division abandoned the advance in order to loot a British supply depot. It had been years since the soldiers had seen equipment of such quality and good food in such profusion.[6]

The effects of Passchendaele were greater than this. The losses suffered there made Britain's manpower shortage all the more acute and also made the Prime Minister more suspicious of Haig than ever. From November on Haig did not get the reinforcements he felt he needed, both because Lloyd George did not trust him and because the General Staff had advised the government that a sizable general reserve was

---

[4] W.O. 106/404, Item 2, W.O. 106/407, Item 45.

[5] Cruttwell, 443, 474–477.

[6] Cruttwell, 476.

best kept at home.[7] Among the reasons given was that it was cheaper to do so.

These decisions were made just at the time when Germany was negotiating a peace with the new Bolshevik government in Russia. The strategic initiative returned briefly to the Germans who were now free to concentrate troops formerly occupied in the East on the Western Front. With these forces, Ludendorff, despite even Hindenburg's doubts and the failure of the submarine campaign, planned a last great offensive which he believed would bring Germany victory before the arrival of American troops in France could prove decisive. Haig rightly guessed that the Germans would attack and that if the attack failed it would be the beginning of the end for them.[8]

The Germans might never even have ventured to attempt another offensive if large American forces had already arrived in Europe. As it was, only four American divisions were in France. The United States entered the war and enthusiastically promised a great deal more than it was able to deliver in the first eight months of its participation. Consequently the period from May until December 1917 was one of disappointment for the Allies. There were so many problems getting the Americans ready to help. First of all, the general problem of Anglo-American relations remained. A long report on this subject was written by Sir William Wiseman in August 1917 and was printed and circulated for the use of the Cabinet. Wiseman felt it necessary to explain the nature of the American political scene in order to prevent misunderstandings between the representatives of the two English-speaking democracies. He assured the Cabinet that Wilson "has the greatest confidence in the future of the Anglo-Saxon race" and saw the necessity for Anglo-American

---

[7] Sir Llewellyn Woodward, *Great Britain and the War of 1914–1918* (London: Methuen & Co., 1967), 322.
[8] Woodward, 324.

cooperation, but Wiseman warned of deep-seated "mistrust of Great Britain . . . kept alive by the ridiculous history books still used in the national schools."[9] England's task, as Wiseman saw it, was "to get enormous quantities of supplies from the United States while we have no means of bringing pressure to bear upon them to this end. . . ."[10] To achieve this purpose he concluded that it was necessary to coordinate Allied demands and to inform the American government ol Allied needs "by sending highly-placed and highly-competent envoys to Washington."[11]

What impressed Wiseman perhaps more than anything else was the interest which America had begun to take in the world beyond its shores, especially the European world. If Britain was careful to direct this interest in the proper direction, she would be able to influence for years to come the "foreign policy of America" which he said "is now in the process of formation."[12]

Besides Anglo-American relations, there was the problem of American mobilization for war. In October Spring-Rice sent a memorandum composed by Lord Eustace Percy which again considered the situation in America. Lord Percy's conclusions were not entirely discouraging, but they were enough to give grounds for pessimism. There was "essential popular unity" in the country about the war but America had failed to make "the same satisfactory progress in industrial organisation for the war."[13] There was no effective organization for dealing with the labor movement and only sheer luck and Secretary of War Newton Baker's skill at negotiating War Department contracts had avoided severe industrial unrest. To make matters worse, Congress had failed to limit "em-

---

[9] F.O. 371/3112/7839, p. 2.
[10] F.O. 371/3112/7839, p. 3.
[11] F.O. 371/3112/7839, p. 3.
[12] F.O. 371/3112/7839, p. 4.
[13] F.O. 371/3123/7827.

ployers' profits"; the excess profits tax had been "whittled down" by the Senate.

Those who represent here the interests of Labour are saying that the United States is possibly the only civilized country where arguments as to "necessary incentives to capital" have still, in many circles, the uncriticized authority of the Ten Commandments . . .[14]

German reports that at the most the Americans would be able to bring 400,000 to 500,000 troops to Europe and that this number was so small that no decisive effect could be expected from it were noted with care in London.[15] The Austrian Intelligence Service was less sure that the Americans could not have a decisive effect. Such matters as the reports that America planned to manufacture and send 20,000 war planes to Europe were taken seriously in Vienna.[16] A few months before this announcement was recorded by the Evidenzbureau, the *London Times'* rather condescending report of the arrival of General Pershing and his staff in England (Saturday, June 9, 1917) was noted in Vienna. The *Times's* report of the naïve American reaction to the uniforms of the Welsh Fusiliers who met them with a guard of honor and to the goat which served as their mascot were duly appreciated in Vienna, along with the significance of Pershing's arrival.[17]

The reports of the British Military Mission in the United States were more pessimistic about American capabilities than those of the k.u.k. Intelligence Service. By September 1917 the need to get American troops into the line even before an entire American Army could be put in the field was being stressed for the sake of bolstering sagging French morale.[18] By October it was clear to the British that the French were waiting for the Americans to come before attempting an

---

[14] F.O. 371/3123/7827.
[15] F.O. 371/3124/7827.
[16] EvB 5784 U.S.A. *Flugwesen* 1917/1918/1919.
[17] EvB 5784 U.S.A. *Heer* 1917.
[18] F.O. 371/3112/27635/184454.

offensive, and it was also more than obvious that the Americans might be a very long time in coming. The Chief of the Imperial General Staff reported with dismay that the Americans had not yet even decided upon what the pattern of their guns should be.[19] In November the effects of the difficulties in Italy and the "Russian situation" caused estimates to appear that on the Western Front the Germans would soon enjoy a superiority of more than 60 divisions. The arrival of American troops was becoming ever more urgent.[20]

There were various reasons for the delay. The French informed London late in December that political considerations caused the Americans to favor National Guard units over the Regular Army, which slowed down training.[21] According to a report issued on January 18, 1918, some of the major reasons for the delay were:

> The false democratic sentiment which places officers and men on an equal footing off parade, the inexperience of officers who fail to assert themselves, and the absence of a non-commissioned officer's class midway between officers and their men.[22]

Nevertheless the Allies were still expecting the Americans to come. On the last day of 1917, the president of the Board of Trade completed a memorandum dealing with the American Army as a "Problem of Imports and Shipping."[23]

How much the Americans were counted on is revealed by a proposal passed along to British GHQ by the chief British Liaison Officer at AEF Headquarters, Lt. Colonel, later Brigadier General, C. M. Wagstaff C.I.E., D.S.O. on December 13, 1917. The suggestion was simple enough. British divisions were short of men but possessed a complete organisational structure. Why not train American battalions or bri-

---

[19] W.O. 106/475 Item 15 Oct. 15, 1917.

[20] W.O. 106/467/9379, American Assistance to the Allies, O.1/132/378.

[21] W.O. 106/474. Report of the French Military Attaché in Washington, 27 December.

[22] W.O. 106/478.

[23] W.O. 32/5165.

gades in British divisions and then, when they were ready, release and send them along to General Pershing, who could form them into American divisions? Apparently the idea had already been presented to General Pershing and his Chief of Staff, Tasker Howard Bliss, but British GHQ considered it a matter of "considerable urgency" and wanted Wagstaff to press the matter.[24] The question of employing American troops with British or French units was to occupy a crucial place in the negotiations of the succeeding months.

The German and Austrian view of the scene was not really substantially different.

After the American entry into the war von Pappus had some encouraging news for the servants of the Wittelsbachs.

M. Kr. 1831

No. 11157   GHQSM   2.6.17

... On 31.5. ... State Secretary Count von Roedern was here along with Mr. von Krupp and Admiral von Hintze, the former ambassador in Peking. These men all agreed with the opinion of the General Staff, that America will not be able in a foreseeable time to send large numbers of troops to Europe, but, [will be able to send] numerous pilots, planes, artillery, material, technicians, etc. Krupp and Hintze believe that America has no intention at all of sending larger units overseas. They think that the main reason for the build up of American forces is the fear of increasing Japanese strength. Japan will always remain America's chief opponent in the battle for the control of the Southern Pacific, for free trade even with America herself, and for the right of unrestricted immigration and settlement there. ...

In America all those people, including the President, who are concerned with politics are said to enjoy only a slight regard. Generally speaking members of Congress can be bought. The American people wish to have nothing to do with the war but because the

---

[24] W.O. 106/490/9347; W.O. 106/466/9379.

"better class" of people hold themselves completely aloof from politics, a few succeed in gaining power for themselves and in exercising it. . . .

5784 Evidenzbureau 1918/1919

Excerpt from the Norddeutsche Allgemeine Zeitung

BERLIN, 1.7.1917

When the United States of America severed relations with us at the beginning of February, the enemy press announced that America would immediately raise an army of 10 million soldiers and send it to Europe as soon as possible, in order to assure the victory of the Allied Powers over Germany. Today almost five months later a commanding general with his staff, and 1,500 soldiers, as well as an American ambulance unit with a strength of 225 men are upon European soil. Only this much of the army of 10 million men is known: that recently the list of the 10 million, who are to be called up, was completed.

Soon after the announcement of the army of millions, the American papers promised that the United States would build a huge fleet of wooden ships which would quickly neutralize the submarine menace. On the 6th of May a French radio broadcast reported that the United States had ordered a thousand wooden ships each of 3,000 tons, which would be finished in five or six months. But on the 25th of May the same radio station reported that the building of wooden ships was an impossibility and the construction of the promised three million tons of shipping space would take at least 18 months. About two weeks ago the American newspapers issued their newest most terrifying report that the United States had decided upon the immediate construction of an enormous airfleet of 40,000 planes which was to be sent to Europe along with the necessary number of pilots in order to assure our opponents the absolute command of the air and to encompass our defeat. In the meanwhile this report has suffered the fate of all the earlier ones. According to a semiofficial statement of the 13th of June it will be necessary to be satisfied with a thousand planes a month. One can only wonder how matters will continue to develop.

The press summaries reported the news of the formal cessation of diplomatic relations between Germany and the United States in early February and did not try to hide the fact that the American government's decision was a popular one. The summary for February 6 states that the American papers left no doubt that their cause was "righteous."

At an important session of the Main Committee (Hauptausschuss) of the Reichstag, a declaration in favor of peace was suggested.

M. Kr. 41

Von Köppel to the Minister of War

No. 6731   GHQSM   7.7.1917

On Friday morning Representative Erzberger unexpectedly presented a suggestion that the Reichstag issue a declaration in favor of peace without annexation or indemnity in the same spirit of unity which had been shown on August 4th, 1914. In view of the great difficulties with the food supply, the fact that the submarine campaign now in its sixth month (including July) had not achieved the promised or hoped for success, and because a year from now we would not get a better peace than today, he argued that such a step was desirable and would be instrumental in achieving peace. He demanded the presence of the Imperial Chancellor and the Army Supreme Command for a discussion of this proposal.[The next day there was a debate.] The Chief of the Imperial Naval Department then defended himself against the reproaches of Representative Erzberger, by denying he had promised that within six months England would be ready for peace! The speakers of the Left (Independent Socialists, Socialists and German People's Party) supported Erzberger's position. The Social Democratic speaker announced that if the resolution should not be passed, there would be a bloody revolution before the year was out.

§   Austria tried to avoid war with America.

VIII 1/19 Kriegsarchiv

K.u.k. Fleet Command to the Commanders of U-boats in the Mediterranean

Ships of the United States of America.

Res. No. 843/Op.   16 July 1917

By order of the Army Supreme Command the agreement of the Imperial German Naval Staff to the following is to be requested with all due courtesy: that, in view of the fact that no state of war exists between Austria-Hungary and the United States of America, Imperial German U-boats, which operate under the k.u.k. flag:

1. will not attack warships of the United States of America;

2. will treat merchant ships of the United States of America as they would vessels of all those states with which Austria-Hungary is not at war.

MAXIMILIAN NJEGOVAN *m.p., Admiral*

§   First reports of the Americans in action.

Personal Affairs of the Württemberg Minister of War. Vol 89.

Reports of the Military Plenipotentiary

No. 8627   GHQSM   27.7.1917

1st Army... Prisoners claim that American troops are to go into action in the Rheims area....

5784 Evidenzbureau 1918/1919

Excerpt from the Norddeutsche Allgemeine Zeitung, *Berlin, 8.12.1917*

All the weak consciences in Germany whom the Entente press

and Wilson's bluff have frightened may be consoled that in the course of the year 1918 the arrival of perhaps a half a million American soldiers at the most can be expected. Since this represents a supply of troops sufficient for one day of heavy fighting, which cannot be replaced after its destruction, it is our firm conviction that the Americans view the entire operation as a training course that will bring their Army the experience of war, if possible without losses, which it urgently requires for subsequent tasks.

§   The English view of America in August 1917.

F.O. 371/3112/7839

> *Printed for the use of the Cabinet. August 1917*
> *Confidential*

I CIRCULATE the annexed memorandum on Anglo-American relations.

Although much of it has already appeared in the notes by Sir W. Wiseman which have been seen by the Cabinet, the paper, as re-written, contains certain new points and is, I think, worth the careful attention of my colleagues. It raises some very important and urgent questions.

R.C.

FOREIGN OFFICE, August, 21, 1917.

MEMORANDUM ON ANGLO-AMERICAN RELATIONS, AUGUST 1917

Our present relations with America present two problems: —

(1) How to assist and encourage the United States to bring the full might of their power to bear upon the struggle as quickly and as effectively as possible.

(2) How to promote a full agreement between the two countries both upon war-aims and terms of peace.

Present Situation:

The situation at present is not satisfactory, for, while the peoples of the United States and Great Britain probably have the same objects in view, there is by no means complete understanding between the two Governments as to the methods that must be employed to gain them.

There is danger of friction in the fact that the high officials of the two Governments are not personally known to each other, and in the normal difficulties of keeping the American authorities fully and constantly informed regarding the changing situation in Europe.

The Government of the United States:

The essential fact to be grasped is that for the purposes of the war the Government of the United States means the personal decisions of President Wilson. The President of the United States is executively almost an autocrat for the period of his term in office, and such a crisis as war considerably increases his power. He can appoint and dismiss his Cabinet at will; and the Cabinet officers are not responsible to Congress, but to the President alone.

Nor does the President entirely depend upon a majority in the Senate or in the House of Representatives. It has happened — as in the last year of Taft's administration — that there was a considerable majority against the President in Congress. Nor need pressure from his party be expected to have much influence since Mr. Wilson cannot in any event be elected for a third term.

Party-feeling in the United States:

But party feeling is very strong to-day. The President is normally a good party man, and it appears that America will run the war on party-lines. For many years after the Civil War the Republican party, with short interludes, remained in power. Towards the end of the Roosevelt administration, and during Taft's administration, the Republicans were drifting out of touch with the mass of the people; but the party-machine was strong and the traditions of the Civil War still made a majority of the people unwilling to place the power of the United States in the hands of the South, *i.e.,* the Democratic party.

President Wilson (particularly since his re-election) may be said to represent a stable majority definitely turned against the more reactionary Republican party, and his personal hold on the Middle West and West (less articulate but possibly more important of opinion than New York and the Eastern States) is very great. The Democrats, moreover, having been out of office so long, are determined not to share authority with their opponents, so that the chances for a Coalition Government seem remote. It is fairly certain that the President will not agree to a Coalition Government unless public opinion, aroused by some important disaster, should force him to do so. Any suggestion of this sort, however unofficial, any press campaign in its favour, however sympathetically conducted, would be a blunder of the first magnitude; for Great Britain, in particular, must avoid any semblance of interference in American domestic politics.

Of the two parties in the United States, the Republicans roughly represent the wealthier and better-educated classes. The Democrats are composed of the gentry of the South, and to some extent represent the rising wealth of the Middle West, but, beyond this, their intellectual outlook is that of the advanced Radical school of thought throughout the United States.

The present Administration is pro-Ally and even pro-English. Two of the members of the Cabinet are said to have been British-born subjects, and all of them have admiration and sympathy for England. It must be remembered, however, that they are bitterly antagonistic to what they imagine to be "Tory England"; and in nine questions out of ten they would be in complete agreement with our advanced Radical party.

President Wilson:

The President himself is of Scotch Presbyterian descent; radical by conviction and training, but opposed to socialism and the undue political power of labour unions. He has the greatest confidence in the future of the Anglo-Saxon race, and believes that the security of the world can best be maintained by an understanding between the democracies of Great Britain and the United States. He has the most bitter and unyielding antagonism to the Kaiser, his form of Government, and anything which might appear to be militarism. He has been long getting into war, but he will not be found to be in a hurry for peace.

United States View of the War:

The people of the United States sincerely believe that they are fighting solely for the cause of human liberty. They see themselves as the only disinterested parties in the war. They believe, too, that they, in participating, will be the deciding factor. Technically, the United States have made war against Germany to protect the rights of Americans, and they are not bound by any of tne Inter-Ally treaties. They reserve for themselves the right to make peace with Germany at any time.

The sentiment of the country would be strongly against joining the Allies by any formal treaty. Sub-consciously they feel themselves to be arbitrators rather than allies.

On the other hand, the people are sincere in their determination to crush Prussian autocracy, and in their longing to arrive at some settlement which will make future wars impossible.

It is important to realise that the American people do not consider themselves in any danger from the Central Powers. It is true that many of their statesmen foresee the danger of a German triumph, but the majority of the people are still very remote from the war. They believe they are fighting for the cause of democracy and not to save themselves.

There still remains a mistrust of Great Britain, inherited from the days of the War of Independence, and kept alive by the ridiculous history books still used in the national schools. On the other hand, there is the historical sympathy for France, and trouble could far more easily be created between the British and the Americans than with any of our Allies. German propaganda naturally follows this line, and has been almost entirely directed against England.

War Aims:

Public opinion will soon force the President to make some more definite statement regarding the concrete aims of the war, and the Allied Governments must be prepared for this. And any pronouncement they can make which will help the President to satisfy the American people that their efforts and sacrifices will reap the disinterested reward they hope for will be gratifying to him, and in its ultimate result serve to commit America yet more whole-heartedly to the task in hand. The more remote a nation is from the dangers of the war the more necessary it becomes to have some symbol or definite goal to keep constantly before it. The Americans are accustomed to follow a "Slogan" or simple formula. The President realised this when he gave them the watchword that America was fighting "to make the world safe for democracy"; but the time has come when something more concrete and detailed is needed.

Practical Difficulties:

Our diplomatic task is to get enormous quantities of supplies from the United States while we have no means of bringing pressure to bear upon them to this end. We have to obtain vast loans, tonnage, supplies and munitions, food, oil, and other raw materials. And the quantities which we demand, while not remarkable in relation to the output of other belligerents, are far beyond the figures understood by the American public to-day.

The Administration are ready to assist us to the limit of the resources of their country; but it is necessary for them to educate Congress and the nation to appreciate the actual meaning of these gigantic figures. It is not sufficient for us to assure them that without these supplies the war will be lost. For the public ear we must translate dollars and tonnage into the efforts and achievements of the fleets and the armies. We must impress upon them the fighting value of their money.

Confusion as to Allied Requirements:

The demands for money, shipping, and raw materials come from the Allies separately and without reference to one another. Each urges that their own particular need is paramount, and no one in America can tell where the next demand will come from and for how much it will be.

The Administration are too far from the war, and have not sufficient information, to judge the merits of these demands. The Allies will have to use patience, skill, and ingenuity in assisting the American authorities to arrive at a solution of this one grave difficulty, which is, in a phrase, "the co-ordination of Allied requirements."

At present confusion reigns not only in the Administration Departments, but in the public mind. There is, on the one hand, a feeling that some of the money and material is not needed for strictly war purposes, and, on the other hand, some genuine alarm is felt that even the resources of the United States will not be able to bear the strain.

German agents at work in the United States have seized upon this situation and are using it to the full. Their activities are aimed at confusing the issues and delaying the time when the full weight and power of America can be brought into the war. They are encouraging the idea that it would be better to conserve American resources for the protection of America, rather than dissipate them in a European quarrel.

Suggested Remedies:

The main remedy for the present state of affairs is to see that the Administration better understand the real state of affairs in Europe, and realise the exact and practical significance of the information which is sent to them from the Allied Governments.

There is a feeling among the British authorities that the President ought to send expert missions to Europe for the purpose of ascertaining the facts and advising him as to the best steps to be taken. Possibly this would be the most practical method, but it is not one which is likely to be adopted. America, and especially the Democratic party, lacks public men who can leave their personal affairs to look after themselves while they travel abroad, even though the call be one of public duty. It can be taken then as certain that the only way to settle any important negotiations with the States is by sending highly-placed and highly-competent envoys to Washington.

Financial Commissioner:

There is, for instance, a very urgent need for an official of the highest standing to proceed to Washington and discuss with Mr. McAdoo financial problems. He should be a man who can not only grasp the strictly financial problems, but who will also understand the political situation in America and can discuss, with the Secretary of the Treasury, the political problems involved in the raising of immense loans in the States. The mistake in the past has been to send purely financial experts who have had little knowledge of, or patience with, the serious political difficulties which face the Administration in Washington.

Then with regard to the four most important supplies, namely: munitions, shipping, oil and food, there should be an official of high reputation in special charge of each: co-operating with, and their work co-ordinated by, the Chairman of the British War Mission. The existing British organisations in the States are admirably suited for the necessary routine work, but in certain cases lack the necessary weight in dealing with the high American officials.

Canada:

In all questions of supplies, financial and otherwise, there must be close co-operation between the British Mission in the United States and the Canadian Government. An imperial representative of position and tact should be appointed to Ottawa to act as liaison between the Canadian Government and the British Mission.

Naval and Military Information:

It is absolutely necessary that the Administration should not only be kept fully informed as to the developments of the military situation, but that care should be taken to see that they understand the information which they receive, and appreciate its significance. For this purpose, it is necessary to have in Washington naval and military officers who have had practical experience in the present war. They should not be considered as naval and military missions for the purpose of instructing the American army or navy, but as "Information Officers" whose duty it would be to receive all the information supplied to the War Cabinet and explain it to the responsible naval and military chiefs in Washington, and to the President himself if necessary, and to obtain from London further information that might be desired on any particular point.

Political Information:

America is for the first time keenly interested in European problems. Americans consider that Washington has become the diplomatic centre of the world. The American people, however, have no great knowledge of European problems, or any fixed ideas as to their settlement. Certain interested groups in America are actively engaged in furthering their own particular cause, but America as a whole has only the vaguest notions of the problems which would face a Peace Conference. America would never for a moment admit that she is prepared to follow the lead of England, but it is nevertheless true that unconsciously she is holding on to British traditions and would more readily accept the British than any other point of view, always provided no suggestion escaped that England was guiding or leading the foreign policy of the United States. It is no exaggeration to say that the foreign policy of America for many years to come is now in process of formation, and very much depends on the full sympathetic and confidential exchange of views between the leaders of the British and American people.

W. WISEMAN

LONDON, August 20, 1917.

§ The Austrian view of the situation in the same month is illustrated by the following report.

VIII- 1/19 Kriegsarchiv

K.u.k. Military Attaché in the Haag

Res. No. 856   31. August 1917

[Lieutenant Colonel Jukowski doesn't believe that England can make good shipping losses caused by the submarine campaign.]

But while England is compelled to use all her shipping to carry on the war, this can not be expected to happen in the case of the Americans.

This is easy to understand when one considers America's attitude towards Japan, and her need not only to maintain her own trade but also to take over those trade routes which England must now give up because she is short of ships. . . .

.   .   .   .   .

. . . submarine warfare, if it continues to be carried on the way it has been so far and even if during the coming winter months there should be far fewer sinkings, is in principle best suited to end the war in our favor. . . .

The Entente can be expected to experience a serious crisis during early 1918 and in the course of the year to realize that it is impossible to continue the war.

The precondition for this result is the continuation of the present submarine campaign. [Jukowski noted that even if the submarines were not quite so successful in the future, the Allied crisis would be delayed only for a few months. He added that Allied resistance depended upon two factors:] the desire of statesmen whose careers are bound to the war as a matter of life and death to continue it on the one hand and on the other the hope that we will collapse before the U-boat warfare forces them to yield. [He also reported that Allied hopes were based upon the news of the internal weaknesses of the Monarchy.] To understand this completely one must live abroad ar 1 hear the reports, especially about political conditions, economic shortages of every sort of raw material, etc. etc. in our Monarchy which are current in informed circles. I really believe that every day at breakfast Lloyd George awaits the news that we have collapsed during the night and that he finds the strength to persevere in this expectation.

§   The first signs of a change in the expectation of what the submarine campaign would achieve were noted by General von Hartz.

M. Kr. 1831

No. 12039   GHQSM   12. August 1917

[Better results were expected in August when new U-boats which have a greater cruising radius would be sent into action. The answer to the plenipotentiary's questions about why the results of the submarine offensive have not quite been what was expected and "in fact remain in general moderate" was that there had been a delay in the production of the new class of submarines.] Otherwise confidence in the success of the U-boat Campaign remains firm. . . .

§   Later in the month von Hartz reported to Munich military dissatisfaction over the behavior of the Parliament.

M. Kr. 1831

No. 12199   GHQSM   26.8.17

Erzberger's role is a particular cause of complaint. GHQ believes that the Parliament did not represent the way people really felt. The parties are said to be trying to exploit the situation "to achieve their selfseeking party aims" [Certain elements at GHQ thought that the Reichstag should be dissolved but von Hartz said that this will not happen. He concluded with a prophetic statement.] Other firebands consider still more radical government measures against the "traitors to the Fatherland" etc. But it is strange that no one considers a revolution in Germany or Prussia possible, not even as a result of the most reactionary, and harshest government measures.

§   Late September appeared to bring some more encouraging news. A report dated September 23, 1917, stated that 230 U-boats were scheduled for production between September and February 1918. However on February 3, 1918, report No. 14246 informed the Bavarian War Minister that due to construction difficulties and delay the date was now September 1918, which was to prove too late.[25]

The first report of the presence of the Americans in the field was made by von Hartz.

M. Kr. 1831

No. 12541   GHQSM   25.9.17

. . . It now appears to have been confirmed that small American units have gone into action south of the Parroy Forest, east of Luneville in formations of the French IX Army Corps.

---

[25] M. Kr. 1831, No. 12521; M. Kr. 1832, No. 14246

§   A few weeks later the news of the first prisoners was brought in.

M. Kr. 1831

No. 13011   GHQSM   3.11.17

... Due to fog and rain there was only light action on the rest of the Western Front: occasional bursts of fire on both sides of Lens and on the Arras-Douai road. Stormtroops of the 1 Bavarian Landwehr Division brought back the first Americans from the trenches close to the Rhine-Marne Canal (10 prisoners, 1 machine gun).

§   The emergence of the United States as a creditor nation was discussed in the following news article on the economic significance of the war.

Evidenzbureau 5784

"The American Creditor" from the Berner Tagwacht, *7.9.1917*

To what extent America has become the creditor of the European states can be seen from a summary of the loans received by the Allies in America which was compiled by the National City Bank in New York. Private bank credits which are reckoned at at least a hundred million dollars are not included in this compilation.

To England	2,086,400.000
To France	1,266,700.000
To Russia	323,500.000
To Canada	334,999.878
To Italy	185,000.000
To Belgium	45,000.000
To Newfoundland	5,000.000
To Serbia	3,000.000

After the war the United States will gradually become the center of international payment settlements.

Evidenzbureau 5784 1918/1919

"The American View of the War" from the Münchner Neueste
Nachrichten

MUNICH, 22 October 1917

Although to date the German public has received a great deal of
information about the way the war was viewed in the United States,
this has been quite inaccurate. It has been confined to newspaper
opinions which as a rule were chosen by friend or foe according to
partisan sympathy, to the various public speeches of statesmen, and
more or less official speakers; and on occasion to accounts of individual visitors to the country, who quite understandably could
report only a portion of what was to be observed. These partial
contributions could never be sufficient to provide a clear understanding of the way Americans thought about the war. At best they
were enough to bring us a deeper understanding of one or another
incident, but they could not give a total picture of the American
psyche during the war, of their views of us, and of the development
which finally ended in the declaration of war. A booklet entitled
America as a Foe, which the director of the Munich Business
School, Professor Dr. Bonn, has just published, fills the gap. The
author, who spent over two and a half years of the war in America,
has been able, as a professor at three American universities and as
an exponent of our affairs, to obtain a thorough knowledge of the
perspective from which the majority of Americans view Germany's
role in the war. . . .

The great riddle which the unfriendly, indeed hostile attitude of
the American world presented to the German public during the first
months of the war, can in no way be completely solved, as Professor
Bonn also convincingly demonstrates, by mere reference to the
kinship between the American ruling classes and the English people.
It is necessary to delve at the roots of the American national character, which is just beginning to develop, in order to understand the
remarkably un-European view of the war in the minds of today's
Americans.

There can be no doubt that one of the major factors which
determines the direction of American opinion is the overwhelming
English influence, which makes itself felt racially, economically,
culturally and politically. The number of immigrants from all the

lands of Europe reaching into millions has not yet been able to erase from the face of the American people and government—taken as a whole—the marks which the English colonists of past centuries have engraved upon it. The professional classes in particular still form a cultural province of old England; the judiciary and the lawyers, the church and the clergy, the educational system and the teachers all breathe an English spirit. They absorb educational material in a constant exchange with England and remold it to fit an American pattern without being able to put aside the inherent British characteristics.

Before the war the economic ties which united America with England were already so close that the links with Germany, which in themselves were not inconsiderable, could not compete with them. Until the heavy indebtedness of the Entente Powers during the war reversed the relationship, London was also the banker for the United States and the British financial world was the provider for a receptive American capital market. But the chains which entwined both have as a result of the indebtedness only become stronger. . . .

Even if these circumstances were sufficient to explain the sympathy of the Americans for England and her allies, they would still not be enough to account for the decided anti-German attitude of the American psyche, if one other factor which is decisive were not added: the pride of the average American in his democratic Constitution. All classes of Americans consider their country to be the birthplace of true civic freedom, of democracy in principle. The form of government is to the American an absolute good, next to which every other kind of constitution, particularly monarchy, is inferior, indeed immoral. This is the reason France, which gave birth to the Revolution, is especially dear to the American, and this is why the 18th Century hostility against the English motherland has given way to the present day affection for England. It is enough for the citizen of the United States to know that democracy as a principle has been realized in his country; he accepts—indeed not trifling—drawbacks with which his democratic national life is connected, as long as his personal freedom, which often turns into licentiousness, remains guaranteed to him. If Germany for example celebrates its extensive social welfare agencies, he has for this only a smile of pity. In the land of perfect democracy, where—at least in theory—no classes exist, everyone can rise as high as he wishes and is able. There is no need for social legislation, for it would only demonstrate the imperfection of the Constitution. For similar reasons the American would rather see some kind of party boss control public affairs even when he is the embodiment of corruption, instead of an incorruptible bureaucracy of civil servants. According to American view the principle of democracy allows no limitation even when accidental human weaknesses pervert it. The same attitude also governs the relationship of the Americans to their President. Once he has become the man chosen by the people, the mass of the citizens support him voluntarily, even if he blunders. The living force of democratic conviction which dwells in the people, at least as an illusion, is the shield which always protects him.

European critics, who examine things impartially, certainly see that in American democracy the principle is often, perhaps even in the majority of cases, an empty illusion, which actually does more harm than good. For all that the major cause of the anti-German tendency in American popular feeling has been just this democratic legend. To him who at least fancies himself to be an absolute democrat a constitutional monarchy of the German kind, of whose nature he has, by the way, only a very vague notion, represents a basic negation of his ideal. Militarism, imperial autocracy, the persecution of the governed by a cast of privileged brutes are the terms in which the average American thinks of German constitutional institutions; and they are sufficient for him to justify a false picture. . . . To a people which is proud of such a Constitution, he attributes every kind of evil, and English atrocity stories have taken good care that there was no shortage of wickedness.

For the American newspaper reader the war has filled the picture frame, which he in his ignorance and democratic self-glorification held out ready for the German people, with a clear picture. The picture matches the frame completely. The German Empire, at all times suspect, appeared to American eyes as the disturber of peace, which desired to realize its dreams of world domination with brutal disrespect for all accepted law. They viewed matters completely differently than we did, because they saw everything only through English eyes. . . . With respect to the invasion of Belgium, the sentence from the Chancellor's speech of the 4th of August 1914 that "necessity knows no law" provided no justification. It was merely an admission of guilt for the violation of the neutrality of a small nation and the breach of a solemnly sworn agreement. According to the American view everything, even the attack upon a neutral country, was ascribed to a political morality which did not shrink from such deeds. He who was capable of this had placed himself outside all political morality and was an alien body in a moral world. England might turn international maritime law upon its head to the detriment of America and the other neutrals, but that weighed little against Germany's Belgian crime, which was viewed as a declaration of war on the entire neutral world. It was impossible to live together with such a country whose excuse that it acted out of necessity could not be believed in view of its military success. No one thought of putting an end to the transport of munitions to the Entente. If Germany was able to draw no war material from America, the responsibility for this did not lie with the Americans. The provision of munitions to the Allies was indeed considered necessary in order to balance Germany's so-called advantage and its suspension would have been viewed as a nonneutral act.

German attempts, in retaliation for the English blockade, to surround England herself with a ring of U-boats could find no real understanding in America. Killing the enemy was considered an absolutely forbidden offense, whether or not for military reasons it was unavoidable. The President, who for internal political reasons had from the beginning supported strict neutrality, fell in his efforts to avoid conflict with all the belligerents into the role of an opponent of that party against which the hostility of the people was announced from the start of the war. After he failed in the Spring of 1915 to stop Germany from continuing submarine warfare, indignation over the sinking of the Lusitania and later of other passenger ships gave him the opportunity to accomplish his ideal. He aimed at that which according to American opinion was alone acceptable: the moral punishment of Germany, for waging submarine warfare. The approaching elections made it appear to him necessary to come before the people with a foreign policy success. Germany's diversion to submarine cruiser warfare was a partial victory for Wilson, which provided the basis for his subsequent diplomatic moves.

What then took place is well known. America saw Germany slipping ever further on a downward path which as it believed an undemocratic country must necessarily follow.... In his book Professor Bonn very correctly notices that in foreign policy — and above all in war—it doesn't matter either whether the things have happened, or how they have happened. It is sufficient for failure or success that certain attitudes concerning them are established and Germany's war policy, or much more the notion which was developed about it, simply could not be fitted into the American world of thought. When towards the end of 1916 Wilson took the initiative to bring about peace, in order to end the unbearable burden caused by English economic warfare and to avoid taking energetic steps against the Entente, he was met by Germany's offer of peace. For a moment Germany's moral prestige in America rose only to fall suddenly to below zero, as the proclamation of unlimited submarine warfare burst into the midst of the discussion over the possibility of peace. The charge of pursuing a Machiavellian policy of which Germany was generally accused was indeed supported by the facts. On top of that came the public announcement of the offer of an alliance to Mexico, which was in the eyes of Americans ultimate proof of political faithlessness, and then finally the Russian Revolution. If in February Wilson still had believed that he would be able to inflict moral punishment upon Germany by severing relations with her, now he could openly enter the camp of those who opposed "German militarism." The Russian Revolution presented a common democratic front against the autocracies of Central Europe and the democratic missionary fanaticism of the average American saw the vision which he had already glimpsed fleetingly at the outbreak of the war reappear clearly before his eyes. The democracies of the world had the holy task of realizing their ideals in the battle against despotism. With this war cry America entered the war.

Of course the statesman Wilson also included in his declaration of war a number of realistic political aims. It was necessary to justify the buildup of American armament and therewith the attainment of American predominance over everyone. This offered the possibility for the strict control of high finance and heavy industry, long one of Wilson's pet ideas, . . . How in particular the American government intends to utilize their country's enormous resources of power for the benefit of the Entente cannot yet be seen clearly but it is beyond any doubt that they intend to throw their weight into the scales with all their might. The description of America's becoming an enemy of the Quadruple Alliance is not a pleasant chapter for the German reader. The modern American is certainly entirely different in his whole intellectual and moral orientation from his European parents and even more so from the German mode of thought. Indeed one of the first tasks of foreign policy is just this: to help an alien people understand one's own way of life, to present them with a conception which fits their own frame of reference, and by constant dealing with them to supplement this essential lesson. That in this respect we have been guilty of sins of omission and serious errors in policy both before and during the war, cannot today be questioned. The precondition for America's joining the Entente was the assumption that she belonged to a common political and cultural community and that this happened at all is due as much to the Entente's own purposeful activity as to our errors. It would be wrong if we believed that we could bring about a friendship with America and thereby conjure up peace overnight by means of a democratization in our own house. But it can in no way damage the general prospect for peace if we now and in the future place more value upon the impression which we make upon other countries in our internal and external relations and not content ourselves with a false self-righteousness, secure in the knowledge that our conscience is clear.

§   The extent of the American commitment to the war worried the Austrians.

Evidenzbureau 5784

News Article on American Airplanes, London Times, 8/10/17

AMERICAN AIR ARMY

VAST SCHEME UNDERWAY

THE 20,000 MACHINES

(FROM OUR CORRESPONDENT.)

WASHINGTON, Oct. 6.

More than 20,000 aeroplanes are now in course of construction in the United States, and this country will soon send the first all-American battleplane to Europe. According to an official statement issued by the Secretary of War, highly satisfactory progress has been made in the equipment of the aerial branch of the Army and in the training of airmen.

While it is inexpedient to impart information of military value, it is permissible to make a partial announcement of the progress of the American aviation programme. Contracts have been allotted and work is in progress on the entire number of aeroplanes and motors for which £ 128,000,000 was provided by the Aviation Bill passed by Congress in July. This called for more than 20,000 aeroplanes. The types of machines now in process of manufacture cover the entire range of training machines, light high-speed fighting machines, and powerful battle and bombing planes of the heaviest design. The contracts cover an ample number of training machines and embrace many giant battleplanes of a capacity equal to the Caproni, Handley Page, and similar types. The American forces in France will be amply equipped with aircraft.

The work of the aviation section has been thoroughly systematized. The training of airmen, the building of motors, the construction of wings are proceeding uniformly, so that when the motors are ready the planes will be ready, and when the finished aircraft are ready the airmen and machine-guns will be available. Within a reasonable time this country will send its first aeroplane to Europe which, from propeller to engine, machine-guns, and camera, will have been made in the United States. Aeroplanes for the United States are being constructed both in this country and abroad. Approximately one-fourth of the number immediately needed will be made abroad.

The United States to-day is in virtual control of many of the materials required for the manufacture of aircraft both for this Government and the Allies. Steps have already been taken for the conservation and distribution of such materials. The aviation service of the Allies may lay claim to "an international general staff" composed of more than 30 air service experts of the Allied nations now in Washington on regular duty with the officers of the American Army and Navy and the members of the Aircraft Production Board. The best 10 experts of the air services of the Allied countries have been lent to this Government in order to aid in getting the American aviation programme under way with the fewest possible mistakes and the greatest economy of time.

There has been a remarkably gratifying response to the call for airmen. The United States has an unlimited supply of young men of courage and self-reliance, of good judgment and decision, for this service, which appeals to the imagination and patriotism of youth. To-day thousands of Americans are being registered for flying. Several great universities are turning out cadets steadily. Twenty-four flying schools have been created. Arrangements have also been made with the Allied countries for the final training of American cadets on foreign soil. These men are being trained in American uniforms and will be turned over as finished airmen to the fighting forces in France. American airmen to-day are training in all the Allied countries and many are undergoing intensive training behind the battle fronts.

The sending of great numbers of American airmen abroad and the acceleration of training preparations at the flying schools in the United States indicate clearly the scope of the Aviation Section since hundreds of millions of dollars have been made available for an army of airmen. There is practically no limit to the number of aerial fighters which the United States can and will furnish in the war for democracy. There exists to-day the closest cooperation among the Allied nations in sending a great aerial fleet above the battle fronts. When the American Army moves up to participate, the fighting eyes will be ready. The signal corps and the staff of foreign advisers are well satisfied with the progress made.

It is not possible to make public all the details of the work accomplished, but the War Department can only say that the earlier expectations and hopes for the consummation of an extensive aircraft programme have been more than realized.

Evidenzbureau 5784

News Article from the London Times *on War Propaganda in the United States of America*

LOAN POST-MARK

AMERICAN GOVERNMENT'S ADVERTISING

The ingenious methods adopted by the United States Government to interest the people in their Liberty Loan have been fully described in messages from America.

We reproduce to-day a special Liberty Loan device which was

largely used during the loan campaign. Stamped on envelopes as a special postmark it could not fail to bring the necessity of subscribing to the loan to the notice of all who received letters.

§   Neutral sources were not all friendly to the United States, as the following articles reveal. This is from a Danish paper.

Evidenzbureau 5784, 30 December, 1917

Berlingske Tidende *of the 12th December 1917*

"FREE AMERICA" DURING THE WAR. I
BY GUDMUNDUR KAMBAN

My two years' stay in the United States coincided with the last 17 months of American neutrality and the first seven months after the declaration of war against Germany—a period in which I had ample opportunity to observe the gradual emergence of the attitude which America now takes.

When the war broke out in 1914, America's only desire was to protect her financial interests. Of all foreigners the Germans were the most respected, while the English were resented just as Americans were looked down upon in England. Although the right to trade with belligerents was guaranteed by the Paris, The Hague and the London Declarations—a right for which America herself fought in 1812—as soon as England limited this right in such a way that it applied only to the Allies, America accepted it for economic reasons. Those who did not profit from the war, sought peace for the moment.

This is the way England plays the game:

All the mail to and from America was to be censored in London.

Washington protests, but does no more.

In the meantime submarine warfare against the United States begins. From the start America supports the English position. The Entente Powers have the absolute right to blockade and starve out the population of Germany, including women and children, but it is an unheard-of outrage to wage war ruthlessly against Great Britain with the help of the U-boat, the only maritime weapon which Germany possesses. The point of view is obvious: a war of starvation waged against Germany does not touch directly American interests, while these same interests are hit very hard by submarine warfare.

The almost endless exchange of notes between the American and German governments and the deterioration of the entire situation are well known.

After the entry of the United States into the war, the war party and the peace party were sharply opposed to each other, but the war party had all the power. Congress and the Press were unanimously behind the President. Despite this, long articles urging the necessity of government action against the many who resist its war plans appeared daily in the newspapers.

§   At the end of the first article there was a note apparently made by the k.u.k. military attaché for the Northern countries. "G. Kamban arrived eight days ago in Copenhagen. He is an Icelander, of good reputation. *Berlingske Tidende* is pro-Entente!"

Berlingske Tidende *of the 13th December 1917*

"FREE AMERICA" DURING THE WORLD WAR (EXTRACT)

II.

War was declared. However the portion of the population which favored neutrality could not with a wave of the hand change themselves into enthusiastic supporters of war. They simply had not had time for this. As late as December 1916 the President's appeal: "Let us keep out of the war!" was to be found on all the street corners of New York, in all the trollies, elevated train lines and subway cars. Later those who supported this desire were invited to write a letter to the President. "Let us keep out of the war!" was a banner around which millions of people gathered.

If however those of that number who still dared, expressed their opinion concerning the war they were immediately silenced. No consideration was given to the fact that a conviction established in the conscience of men for two and a half years could not be replaced in a few weeks by an entirely contrary one. Enormous fines and jail sentences were imposed upon those who dared to speak against the war. The government's orders were executed with a harshness that, with the exception of old Russia, hardly finds a parallel among the other belligerents.

.   .   .   .   .

In America freedom is granted to him, who has enough money so that he need not complain about anything. What an advantage this is compared to other countries!

.   .   .   .

On the 10th of August there was an article in the Philadelphia Public Ledger (the newspaper in which Mr. Gerard wrote of his experiences in Germany) which implied that the government had executed secretly several labor agitators. The newspaper defended this mode of procedure and stated that the only reply to a truely hostile act was the bullet. . . . " The punishment for any treason was death."

And as if the government did not treat the defenders of freedom of speech harshly enough, these even ran the risk of being murdered illegally and unjustly in the name of patriotism by their fellow citizens.

A man named Frank Little, a weak cripple, but an ardent enthusiast, made a speech against the war in August and maintained that the Draft Law of the 18th of May 1917 was unconstitutional. A little later six masked men took him away from his apartment at night in an automobile and several days later his body was found in the woods.

One man dared to publish an excerpt from the American Declaration of Independence as a leaflet. As a result of a printing error the quotation marks in one of the paragraphs were left out. The judge,

Mr. Murphy, assumed that the paragraph had been written by the publisher and condemned the man to 90 days in jail for treasonous activity; it was termed "treasonous and revolutionary" in the sentence.

The offense of speaking against the war is often so severely punished that several of the judges have already destroyed the "moral" effect of the maximum penalty by using it so often. A young man named Louis Kramer spoke openly against the Draft which began on the 5th of June, and was condemned by the judge (Julius Mayer) to two years in prison and a fine of 10,000 dollars. One doesn't need to know anything about American prisons to be indignant about such a judgment.

It must be admitted that a person may speak more freely should he be the possessor of several million dollars. The so-called Newspaper King and multimillionaire, Mr. Hearst, who has repeatedly said in his newspapers that the people should vote on whether or not war should be declared, has merely been labeled as pro-German, but neither imprisoned nor hanged.

On the other hand the well-known anarchist, Emma Goldmann, and her supporter, Alexander Bergmann, were thrown into prison, because they said the same thing which Mr. Hearst wrote. Her friends were able to appeal successfully to the Supreme Court and to obtain her release by paying a high bail. But the government continues its persecution under the leadership of the District Attorney, Harold Content; . . . .

The movement has extended to areas which have nothing to do with the war, to art, to literature, to languages. Many schools have banned instruction in German. The Chicago opera has fired all German singers and has cut all German music out of its program. The same would have happened at the Metropolitan Opera in New York, if one of the directors, Otto Kahn, whose firm, Kahn, Loeb & Co. has at various times provided the Allies with war loans and whose favorite composer is fortunately Wagner, had not opposed it. On the other hand one doesn't dare sing a German song at home.

The Scandinavian countries are viewed with ever-increasing coldness and the newspapers describe America's export restrictions as a well earned punishment for the "limitless greed" of these countries.

Only one New York paper protested against the enactment on July the 15th of the law restricting exports. The Newspaper King, Mr. Hearst, wrote on July the 11th in the *New York American:*

Our government now intends to issue an embargo law against Switzerland, Holland and Scandinavia in order to starve these neutral countries and to force them to help with the blockade against Germany. . . . A few months before Mr. Lansing, the Secretary of State, protested in Mr. Wilson's name against such a blockade of neutral countries and of Germany, as fundamentally "illegal and irresponsible."

These are the exact terms which Mr. Lansing used in his last protest against England's blockade of Germany and neutral countries. . . . It is difficult to understand how the blockade against neutrals in the years 1915 and 1916 was illegal and irresponsible and in the year 1917 is legal and permissible.

Last September it was certainly no advantage in America to be a Swede. Henning Berger's piece, "The Flood," was played in a Broadway theater, an honor which is seldom granted to a Scandinavian work even though the level of the New York theater is rather low. The play was warmly received. A few days later the "Swedish Affair" was made public and the owners had to close the theater immediately.

GUDMUNDUR KAMBAN

CHAPTER V

The Grand Tour Continues

§ Early in January Wilson delivered his Fourteen Points Address to the Congress.[1] The Fourteen Points were destined to be more honored in the breach than in the practice, but the principles they represented were to play an important role in the propaganda war waged by the Allies in the ensuing months. Before the year was out even Ludendorff was to appeal to them as a basis for peace, but there is no evidence that he had ever read them. In the same month Sir Cecil Spring-Rice asked to be relieved and was replaced in Washington by Lord Reading, who did appear to get on better with the Americans. Sir Cecil died in Ottawa on February 16, 1918. He had served the Allied cause well but there was still much to be done.

Since November Ludendorff had been planning his offensive, which might better be described as a series of massive assaults on the Allied lines. The Allied Command was under no illusions about what was to come. As Robertson, the Chief of the Imperial General Staff, saw the matter, the American Army constituted the last major reserve of manpower which the Allies could count on to meet the German threat. The chief concern of the British and the French

---

[1] Daniel M. Smith, *The Great Departure: The United States and World War I, 1914–1920* (New York: John Wiley & Sons, 1965), 94.

was to get as many Americans overseas, into the line, and, if possible, under their own command, as could be arranged. This of course involved shipping over a great number of men, and the question was whether the troops should come in divisional units or priority should be given to, say, infantry or machine gunners. General Pershing wanted divisions; the British in particular wanted infantry for their own divisions.

The negotiations between Pershing, the Allied Command and the American government filled the reports of the next months. As was already obvious from the negotiations of December 1917, the British were worried. On January 10 Robertson wrote to Pershing:

> The British divisions are being reduced from 12 to 9 battalions because of the shortage of men. . . . There are already 28 more German divisions on the West Front than a year ago; there are 11 fewer British and French.
> I trust that the above explanation makes everything clear, . . .[2]

Wagstaff cynically suggested agreeing to bring the Americans over in divisional formations and then, when the emergency arose, breaking up the divisions and employing the American infantry battalions in British divisions.[3] As Wagstaff said, "When the men are here, invent an emergency, and use the men." Wagstaff believed that two American corps on the Western Front were enough to satisfy "Yankee" national sentiment, "provided they wave their flag hard enough."[4]

Everyone seemed to have his own plans for the Americans. Haig's headquarters had a plan, the C.I.G.S. had another, and Pershing, who after all spoke for the Americans, was thinking of something quite different. All the discussions caused real pessimism. In a memorandum to the War Cabinet concerning American battalions for British divisions, written on January 10, Robertson expressed little hope:

---

[2]W.O. 32/5165/8701.
[3]W.O. 106/490/9347, 13.1.18.
[4]W.O. 106/490/9347.

I have never been very sanguine as to American assistance in any form this year. . . . [he felt the American preparations were going very badly.] . . . she is doing very badly. . . . she has never made any real study of war organization; . . . The French have lost all patience, and their relations with the Americans are the reverse of good.[5]

The Prime Minister appealed to Colonel House on January 15 for 150,000 infantrymen, which the British were willing to bring over and supply, if they could be assigned to British divisions for six months. The argument was that it took less shipping space than to bring over a fully equipped division and less time to train smaller units once they arrived.[6]

Finally, early in February an agreement was reached. The British would sacrifice food supplies to bring over an extra 150,000 men, as well as the 12,000 men a month who formed part of the normal American divisional formations. The 150,000 men would "consist of the personnel of six American divisions, namely about 90,000 infantry (72 battalions) and 60,000 to 70,000 men of other arms. . . ." The crux of the agreement was that the infantry was to serve with British divisions for training purposes and that the British would bring over the rest of the men to complete the divisional personnel to please Pershing. After training, the infantry would be returned to Pershing.[7] Of course training took a long time and an emergency might well change this agreement. The agreement caused problems, for early in March elaborate negotiations were still being carried out about American troops assigned to British units. They were to receive the same rations "with the exception that coffee should be substituted for tea."[8]

The agreement also reflected other considerations. Like the

---

[5] W.O. 106/490/9347.

[6] W.O. 106/490/9347.

[7] W.O. 32/5165/8701, January 30, 1918, Robertson to Pershing, January 31, 1918, Pershing to Robertson.

[8] W.O. 106/465.

French, the British were nearing the end of their strength. They knew that ultimately the Americans would play the decisive role in the war, though it was generally believed this would not occur before 1919 or 1920. A subsequent appraisal summed it up very well. "As the War goes on the offensive power will pass to the American Army. . . ."[9] Reluctantly but realistically they made the compromises believed necessary for victory. Black Jack Pershing had his way, and American national feeling was not offended by the sight of the doughboys serving under a foreign flag.

The great German offensive of March 21 changed everything. It was the first of a series of major assaults upon various sectors of the Allied line which were to continue until July 15. In March and early April the lines in front of the old Somme battlefield were breached by the great "Michael" offensive, but the Germans failed to take Amiens and to separate the British Army from the French. Then on April 9 came the attack in Flanders along the Lys River which failed to push the British back to the Channel ports. At the end of May 27, the Germans struck in the south across the Chemin des Dames ridge. American and British warnings of the coming attack were not heeded by General Duchêne, the local commander, and his combined French and British force suffered a terrible fate. Paris seemed threatened as the Germans drove along between the Marne and the Ourcq toward the city, but they were never able to push quite far enough. The July 15 attack that was the final German effort pushed to the southwest across the Marne, but this time a French defense in depth stopped it before it could become really dangerous. Ludendorff had to give up his plan for a last great blow in Flanders, "Hagen."

On July 18 the Allies counterattacked against a weakened German Army which was now hardly able to bear the stress

---

[9] W.O. 158/20 General Staff Notes, File 4, Item 145, January 1917–22/10/18.

of a series of bloody defensive battles. Despite Russia's defeat, the German situation even before the March offensive had been grim. Cruttwell believes that if they had stayed on the defensive during 1918 the Germans might have won a better peace from Wilson in 1919.[10] This is a question that can never be answered. Due to the blockade, Germany was beginning to starve by the end of 1917. It may well have been the case that only the hope that victory might come from the great offensives in the spring kept her fighting so long. Ernst Jünger describes what it was like to fight on after the great offensives had failed in terms of continuing to struggle as duty required but "without hope."[11]

The situation which Ludendorff faced by August 1918, especially after August 8, the "Black Day" of the German Army, when the British, Canadians, and Australians had broken into the great German salient before Amiens, was really hopeless. In fact it was the same situation which he had faced in November 1917 when it was clear the submarine campaign had failed, but this time his last reserves were gone and he faced an enemy who was being reinforced at a rate which no one had imagined possible even five months before. Ludendorff had always maintained that Germany must either gain a military victory or face defeat. His attempt at victory had brought her a military defeat.

All his technical skill had not sufficed. Bruchmüller's artillery tactics, the magnificent *Angriff Divisionen* (attack divisions) with their Stormtroops, and the new techniques of advance were all in vain, in part because Ludendorff himself had not thought beyond the problem of punching a hole in the Allied line.[12]

---

[10] C.R.M.F. Cruttwell, *A History of the Great War, 1914–1918* (Oxford: Clarendon Press, 1934), 505.

[11] Ernst Jünger, *Werke, Tagebücher* (Stuttgart: Ernst Klett Verlag, no date), I, 314.

[12] Peter Graf Kielmansegg, *Deutschland und der Erste Weltkrieg* (Frankfurt: Akademische Verlagsgesellschaft Athenaion, 1968), 633–634.

The very fact that his forces did punch several holes in the Allied line but could not follow up their success reflects a basic flaw in Ludendorff's strategic concept which lacked a coherent aim, and it too led to a major catastrophe for Germany.

Faced with defeat, the Allies had called for help and America had answered the call. On March 24 the British representative in the Hague asked for information about the extent of the German success and some kind of news concerning the panic which the Germans claimed their artillery barrage had caused.[13] The request reflected the gravity of the situation. It was decided at Versailles on March 27 that to save France, American infantry and machine gun units were essential.[14] The next day Lloyd George cabled Lord Reading in Washington that Foch had been appointed to coordinate the Allied defense against the German attack and told him to explain to President Wilson "the paramount importance of sending American troops to France with the utmost speed."[15] The cable continued with a request that Reading persuade Wilson to agree that all units sent during the emergency be "brigaded for the duration of the crisis with French or British divisions." The message closed with a confidential paragraph which ended:

I doubt if it is realized that unless the U.S.A. throws everything she can into the battle now the war will probably be decided without her having made any substantial contribution to the actual fighting.[16]

On the 30th of March another urgent message was sent demanding 120,000 American infantry a month. It closed with the words, "We rely upon you to see that these obstacles are not allowed to hinder the transportation of these vital troops, otherwise the consequences may be disastrous."[17] On April 1 the Prime Minister's tone was even more urgent:

---

[13] F.O. 371/3441/53611.
[14] F.O. 371/3441/56053/f. 54202.
[15] F.O. 371/3441/7862.
[16] F.O. 371/3441/7862.
[17] F.O. 371/3441/7862.

The President must overrule at once the narrow obstinacy which would put obstacles in the way of using American infantry in the only way in which it can be used to save the situation. If she fails disaster is inevitable. . . .[18]

Lloyd George added some additional thought on the matter on April 2: "I believe that the German chances now depend mainly upon whether or not America can get her troops effectively into the line in time."[19] The "obstacle" and creature of "narrow obstinacy" was Pershing, as a cable sent on April 8 to Lord Reading revealed. "Pershing's views are absolutely inconsistent with the broad policy which we believe the President has accepted." The same day Lloyd George promised the Belgians Tunbridge Wells as an exile capital.[20] The Prime Minister was becoming desperate. On April 9 he cabled to Reading that if the Americans didn't arrive,

. . . we cannot be answerable for the consequences . . . all questions of building up an independent American Army in Europe must come second to this imperative necessity while the crisis lasts.

On April 14 he stated, "There can be little doubt that victory or defeat for the Allies depends upon the arrival of American infantry."[21]

Pershing was unmoved. He wanted his own army and he never agreed to relinquish American troops for more than a short period. The minutes of the War Cabinet meeting held on April 9 revealed the British view of Pershing's attitude:

. . . Summing up the attitude of General Pershing, General Whigham added that he had created in his mind the impression that General Pershing wanted to make a United States Army instead of helping us during the critical summer months.[22]

Secretary Baker would have been more generous, but Persh-

[18] F.O. 371/3441/57430/f. 54202.
[19] F.O. 371/3441/7862.
[20] F.O. 371/61508/54202; 62450/f. 54202.
[21] F.O. 371/62450/f. 54202.
[22] W.O. 106/490/9347 War Cabinet, 387.

ing was the man on the spot. The best the Allies could do was to arrange a new agreement which called for the transportation of infantry units to France and allowed for a substantial period of training with British units, for which the British agreed to pay by providing artillery when the American units were formed into divisions. This was to compensate for the American, i.e., Pershing's, willingness to send infantry and machine gunners and not complete divisions.[23]

By June, despite Foch's low opinion of American troops, it was decided to let Pershing have his way. A memorandum from the Deputy Director of Military Operations dated the 29th of June explained why. The Americans had begun to realize the value of their "untrained" troops compared to those of "veteran French divisions." They believed that they would soon be fit to "operate as an American Army." The memorandum argued further that "It is no more use our trying to keep them back in our divisions. . . ."[24] Several other factors influenced this decision. At the beginning of June the Supreme War Council had come to an important decision. To win the war an American Army of 100 divisions was necessary. Victory was impossible without it:

It is impossible to foresee ultimate victory in the war unless America is able to provide such an army as will enable Allies . . . to establish numerical superiority.[25]

To start with the Allies had called for the Americans to send over 250,000 men in June and July.[26] The request was met and Germany's hopes for victory or a negotiated peace favorable to her were doomed.

The beginning of the New Year at Supreme Headquarters was marked by internal conflict. General von Hartz reported

[23] W.O. 106/490/9347 Memorandum, 20.4.18.
[24] W.O. 106/1513/94131 29.6.18.
[25] F.O. 371/3441/98597/f. 54202.
[26] F.O. 371/3441/98597/f. 54202.

the difference of opinion between Major General Hoffmann in the Eastern command and Ludendorff over the question of the Polish border to General von Hellingrath on January 6.[27]

The Evidenzbureau (5784) cited the German *Militär-Wochenblatt,* which in turn quoted Swedish sources, on the American Army. The Americans were just beginning to organize and train their Army. For the moment the Americans posed no threat.

Evidenzbureau 5784

1918 — Militär-Wochenblatt *— No. 93, page 2302*

THE ARMY OF THE UNITED STATES

The "Stockholms Dagblad" (19.1 and 24.1) writes:
The operative units, which have been formed from the Regular Army and consist of about four or five infantry corps, may have been brought over to France already. The Cavalry appears to be composed entirely of new units formed by the Regular Army. The 15 peacetime cavalry regiments have been increased to 25, and apparently the intention is to organize these in an independent cavalry corps. The cavalry of the National Guard has been converted into machine gun units. By an order of the President the National Guard, . . . has been merged with the Regular Army. From these and from volunteers, as well as from a portion of the draftees from the National Army, 17 infantry corps have been formed which are numbered 26–42. The 16 corps of the National Army bear the numbers 76–91. A negro corps is to be added later to this Army.
One has to count both the National Guard and the National Army. The organization of both groups seems to follow the same lines. In addition, in case voluntary enlistments decline, it is planned to supplement the units of the National Guard with draftees. The difference between the groups will probably be abolished completely. The first difficulties to be overcome were the lack of cadre troops and a shortage of quarters.

---

[27] M. Kr. 1832, No. 13863, 6. January, 1918.

When the buildup of the army was first begun 10,000 officers were available; the majority of these had very little training. The creation of 16 officer training camps was ordered in April. In the middle of May the first course was begun; 27,000 candidates were graduated on the 15th of August. A new course was held between the 27th of August and the 26th of November and another one will begin in January. Beyond this several thousand N.C.O.s from the old Regular Army have been made officers. A great number of people have also received officer's commissions in order to occupy special posts. As far as numbers are concerned the Officer Corps seems to be well provided for and also appears to possess sufficient reserves to cover the losses of the first period in the field. Their quality, however, remains another question. It is simply impossible to make men, who have had no previous training, field officers within three months and still less possible to make them suitable leaders for the task of training recruits, even if they are the best qualified human material. Besides, there is no reason to assume that the average American possesses in this respect greater potential than for example the Swede; the contrary is more likely. On account of the shortage of good instructors, the training cannot have been the best possible. Even the professional officer in America is not prepared for the job of modern recruit training. Nevertheless, French and English instructors are available. However there seem to be only a few of them and in any case their activity will obviously be limited due to American jealousy. Battle training seems mainly to have trench warfare in mind.

As evidence of what an important place the new officers, despite their summary training, must take in recently formed units, mention is made of the fact that in an infantry regiment of 103 officers only the commander, the three officers of the regimental staff and one major were regulars. During the summer, 33 large training camps were set up, one for each new infantry corps. Each camp contains 40,000 men. The camps are spread out all over the United States and are named after American Military leaders. A corps will be trained in each camp. It is possible to conclude from this distribution and the statement that the strength of an infantry regiment is 103 officers and 3652 men, that the organization of a corps for battle will be 12 infantry battalions supported by 12 field and 6 heavy batteries.

The National Army began to report for duty in these camps on the 5th of September; in some camps joining up has been temporarily delayed, because the barracks have not been completed. The National Guard went into its training camps during the autumn. A conflict between the central government and the officials of the various states began, because the former, in order to achieve a uniform organization, merged National Guard regiments with each other and thus threatened their rather capricious peacetime organization. It was believed by the states, with justification, that this would destroy the military tradition of the National Guard. Finally an abrupt order issued by the President on the 22nd of October forbade the commanders of former National Guard units to make any complaints to federal authorities about the reorganization.

In addition to divisional formations a large number of special units appear to have been established. It is noteworthy that the first battalion to be instructed in the use of such essential weapons as gas and flamethrowers was only trained in the middle of October. Present reports do not give evidence of larger tank formations. Armored cars, probably of a simpler type, had already been ordered by the American War Department before the war. The air arm is an entirely separate formation.

At the outbreak of the war the War Department planned to form a professional flying corps with a complement numbered in four figures. The construction of 22,000 airplanes, including 2,000 training machines for the flying school, was sanctioned, and great pains were taken to draw upon the war experience of the Allies. Already on the 20th of March last year a commission came to Europe to study aviation both at and behind the front. An international air staff, to which 30 outstanding English and French experts belong, was formed in Washington.

The enlistments of pilot candidates, particularly from sport-loving student circles, seem to be very numerous. Before they are accepted as pilots, the candidates are examined as to their suitability for the profession. Those who are suitable are sent to a pilot's school, where they are given the necessary military training, knowledge of motors, and theory of flying. This course lasts two months. After the examination, further training takes place at an airfield. It is not clear how long this actual flight training lasts; apparently at the most a half a year. The United States has at present 24 large training camps for pilots, besides at least two American aerodromes in France.

At first the manufacture of airplanes seems to have run into major difficulties. Radical means were employed to encourage it, for example: the suspension of all patents. A quarter of the number of planes sanctioned will be obtained from abroad. Nothing as yet is known of the tactical organization. It is too early to judge the new American Air Force. The experience of the European combat theaters teaches that the air arm is an area in which real effectiveness is extremely difficult to achieve, and above all the quality of the general military training of the personnel plays a very important role in the matter. It can hardly be assumed that the improvised American Air Force will achieve a high quality before it has experienced the true tempering of the school of war.

§   America's potential as an economic threat was not ignored.

Evidenzbureau 5784 1918/1919

Report of the k.u.k. Military Attaché at the Hague, 24.2.1918

A spy has learned from a Dutch wholesale merchant who is in contact with London firms that during the last month various North American firms have opened branch offices in London. It is said that this has been done in order to gain a more favorable position in the European market after the war. The English business community appears to wish to combat penetration by such competition immediately and has entrusted the former Minister of Trade, Runciman, with a mission in connection with the matter.

Evidenzbureau 5784 1918/1919

Professor Sänger, the editor-in-chief of the *Neue Rundschau* in Berlin, made the following statement about Anglo-American relations after he had returned from a political mission in Copenhagen.

Sänger believes England had already realized in 1915 that she must share her position of world domination with America, because it was impossible for her to maintain it alone in the old way. It is incorrect to assume that there will be rivalry between these two states as a result of America's growth. Sänger is convinced that an intimate Anglo-Saxon Alliance, whose economic provisos and political spheres of influence have already been agreed upon, will develop and enable the two countries to rule the world jointly, chiefly through the control of raw materials, trade routes, and the other markets which are at least indirectly under Anglo-Saxon influence. Should Germany fail to protect adequately her access to world markets at the peace negotiations, she would within a few years face an unavoidable decline to the point of real misery, even if her military strength appeared to be superior. The entire war, which was primarily the result of economic factors, will also be decided by economic weapons. It would be a good thing if the German people were informed of these matters not only in the press but also by the government itself. Seen from an economic point of view it is possible to understand why the Entente, which has been beaten militarily everywhere, still shows inner confidence and seems able to make entirely impossible demands which, when observed superficially, befit only the military victor.

.   .   .   .   .

With respect to Canada, Sänger believes that this country will in due time undoubtedly be ceded to the United States in return for some kind of clever concessions to England. Canada's wheatland is already one of America's best investments.

NORDSON

Hopes of labor unrest or even revolution in America were not lightly put aside by the Central Powers.

27.5.18 k.u.k. Foreign Ministry, Evidenzbureau 5784
Res. 14572 No. 8   9 March 1918

THE PRESENT STATE OF
THE SOCIAL DEMOCRATIC MOVEMENT IN AMERICA

In order to assess properly the influence of the war and the

Russian Revolution upon the American working class, the fact must be kept in mind that revolutionary labor movements threatened the economy of the United States before America's entry into the war (the Colorado strikes of 1913 and 1914, the great New Jersey strike of 1915). When in August 1916 the Railway Worker's Union (one of the great brotherhoods) sought to force the legalization of the eight-hour day by a sudden strike ultimatum, this burning labor question may well have become one of the main reasons for America's entry into the war. The captains of industry hoped that the war would bring about a stricter organization of America's political and economic structure. American workers have as yet failed to carry their social struggle into the political sphere. They have limited themselves to the organization of unions, to the battle for higher wages, etc. Only a small portion of the American working class is organized. Along with this organized working class there is a large torpid mass of unorganized workers. This group consists mainly of non-English speaking foreigners and forms America's helots.

Besides these two large groups two separate movements of noticeable intellectual influence require mention. These are: American Socialism and the so called I.W.W. movement (Industrial Workers of the World). It can be said that only members of these two groups carry on class-conscious revolutionary propaganda and that the repressive activity of the American government is directed solely against them. American Socialism cannot be compared with the great Socialist parties of Europe. It has no influence upon the unions and has aroused strong protest from the American middle class by inscribing pacifism upon its banner. Its surprisingly great success in the last municipal and state elections (in November 1917) has caused general consternation. As a result the government has taken sharp countermeasures (forbidding newspapers, etc.). However most intensive efforts are being made to transform the Socialist Party into a middle class party for the elections in the fall of 1918. If American Socialism can be attributed to German and Russian influence, then the I.W.W. movement can be traced back to Russian, Italian and French sources. The I.W.W. members lead strikes and with great success; they have been greatly impressed by the example of Bolshevism with its land distribution and confiscation of capital. This explains the stern measures of the American authorities against this revolutionary movement. All the newspapers and organizational cen-

ters of the I.W.W. movement were suddenly seized; the most important leaders were arrested and prosecuted. American public opinion
compares this persecution with lynch justice. Due to the present
isolation of the country very little more could be learned. The
I.W.W. movement seems to be broken up. The freedom of movement of the Socialists has been substantially checked; nevertheless
the growing dissatisfaction of organized labor represents a very
serious threat and it seems sure that the approaching fall elections
will bring about very profound and hazardous shifts of power within
the United States.

§   The British also watched the Socialists and I.W.W. with
care. They too sensed potential danger as Colville Barclay's
report to the Foreign Secretary, The Right Honorable A. J.
Balfour, reveals.

F.O. 371/3492/7871

No. 347   BRITISH EMBASSY, WASHINGTON, May 3rd, 1918

SIR,
    With reference to my despatch No. 241 of March 27th in which I
alluded to the apparent split in the Socialist party on the question of
America's participation in the war, I have now the honour to report
that this movement in [sic] increasing in strength and significance.
    As previously stated, the St Louis platform of the Socialist party
adopted last April was definitely anti-war in character. This attitude
was based on the majority report of the Convention. A minority
report was also drawn up by John Spargo, who declared that the
cause of civilization required the triumph of the Allies in the present
war. It was ignominiously rejected at the time but has since become
the focus for the growing movement away from the St Louis platform. Lately there have been several indications of a decided change
of outlook in the Socialist party.
    Spargo, in a letter to the press on the subject of the so-called
International, has proposed that before any Convention of this body
can take place, a meeting should be held of all Socialists who are

opposed to the attitude adopted by the Socialists of Germany and Austria. Not long ago Mr. Hoan, the Socialist Mayor of Milwaukee, a strong Socialist centre, announced that the platform of his party had become inconsistent with his oath of office as Mayor. He offered to resign either from the party or from his office. The County Central Committee of the Socialist party, however, unanimously decided to support the Mayor in carrying out his official duty and also to retain him as a member of the party. The Jewish Socialists and the Bohemian Socialists have both passed resolutions in favour of supporting the Government in the prosecution of the war. The seven Socialist Aldermen of New York, of whom the leader is Algernon Lee, have changed their attitude towards the Government's War Loans and voted for the Third Liberty Loan. They attribute their change to the conduct of Germany towards the Russian Revolution. Former leaders of the party, such as Spargo, Stokes, Russell and Walling, refuse to be identified with the St Louis platform and are drifting towards the new National Party.

Meanwhile, the pacifist and anti-conscriptionist elements have also been organizing: On May 4th a meeting is to be held by members of what is known as the Young Democracy and a campaign will be started to run anti-conscriptionist candidates for local offices. The members of this body are mostly young college students and at present its influence is insignificant.

Even the situation among the I.W.W. seems to be undergoing an improvement, although there are at present 112 members of this body awaiting trial in Chicago on charges of opposition to military service and of propaganda for the promotion of strikes to hold up the production of war materials and especially of spruce. Colonel Disque, who was deputed by the War Department to take charge of the spruce production, is responsible for the improvement in the attitude of the I.W.W. in the North West. By means of a loyal labour league started by himself, he has succeed [sic] in gaining the confidence of many members of the I.W.W. who have enrolled themselves in this body. And at a meeting at which nearly 62,000 of the league were represented an agreement was come to which promises to satisfy both parties.

The country, however, appears to consider that more adequate steps should be taken to deal with the labour situation if the full efficiency of the United States is to be put into the production of war

supplies. The fear of organized obstruction has been especially noticeable in the Senate where it has crystalized round two measures,
an amendment to the Sabotage Bill (see my despatch No. 340 of
May 1st) by which it was sought to make it an offence to go on strike
in any essential war industry, and a bill introduced by Senator
Chamberlain intended to put all trials for espionage or alleged enemy
activity under courts martial instead of the civil courts. Both these
measures, however, failed, the first being defeated in the Senate on
the ground that it would make all strikes illegal, and the second was
dropped by its introducer in consequence of a letter from the President to Senator Overman (copies of which I have the honour to
enclose) in which Mr. Wilson pointed out that the effect would
practically be to introduce Prussian militarism into the United
States. Although these rather drastic remedies have not been attempted, it is hoped that under the Overman Bill, which has passed
the Senate and awaits passage by the House, the Administration will
receive powers to carry out a more unified labour policy on the lines
laid down in the report of the War Labour Conference Board (see
my despatch No. 226 of April 4th).

I have the honour to be, with the highest respect, Sir, your most
obedient, humble servant,

(For the Ambassador)

COLVILLE BARCLAY

§   However the main concern of the British government
during the early spring of 1918 was to convince the Americans that they must send reinforcements as soon as possible
to Europe.

F.O. 371/3441/7862

To Lord Reading
Secret and Confidential. Following from Prime Minister

No. 1887   2.4.18

I want to impress upon you, in order that you may press it upon

President Wilson and the administration, the supreme importance of time in the matter of American reinforcements. This battle is only at its first stage. We have survived the first crisis but there is bound to be another attack very shortly, but if we defeat the second there will be a third and so on until one side or other is exhausted or the winter puts an end to the fighting. The closest analogy to the present struggle is the battle of Verdun but fought on a vastly larger scale and with the whole Western front from Flanders to Venice as the theatre. In the stage of the 1918 campaign now beginning the enemy probably reckons for his success on refitting his divisions faster than the Allies and on outlasting them in man-power. He will, therefore, go on delivering blow after blow until he has got a decision or is exhausted.

It is very difficult for you at this distance, without being in close touch with the realities of the position, to realise how success or disaster in this battle will be decided by the exertions which America puts forth in the next few weeks or even days. I believe that the German chances now depend mainly upon whether or not America can get her troops effectively into the line in time. The difference of even a week in the date of arrival may be absolutely vital. In this contest an advance of a week in the arrival of troops may win a battle, and the delay of a week may lose it. And remember that no troops can be put into the battle line for at least a month after they land. They must be put through the final training by men acquainted with the conditions at first hand and this, I understand, is alone possible in France.

We have so often had large promises in the past, which have invariably been falsified in the result that I am sincerely apprehensive that this last undertaking may not be carried out in actual practice. In these circumstances everything depends upon your going beyond the ordinary province of an ambassador, and exercising personal supervision over the carrying out of the pledge. The War Mission of which you are the head will enable you to find out where delays are occurring. Immediately a hitch does occur we rely upon you to bring pressure to bear in the right quarter to secure its immediate removal. In particular we depend greatly on Colonel House and hope that he will devote his great influence and energy to this question until it is certain that 120,000 American infantry are going, in fact and not merely on paper, to arrive in Europe in April, and in each succeeding month afterwards. If you can get more so much the better. We can do with all you can send. I am told that there are barely 400,000 infantry in all in the whole of the United States with which to enable President Wilson to redeem his pledge of sending 480,000 men. If so, it is essential that there should be an immediate fresh draft on a large scale.

In order to facilitate your task I am sending over Mr. Graeme Thomson by the first boat.

German Foreign Ministry 21/380

3.4.1918

[The German military attaché in Bern reported good news. The Austrian military attaché had told him that in American Catholic circles there was a peace movement underway. The rest of his report concerned war weariness in America.] The Americans are beginning to recognize that, all their size and power, do not adequately compensate the Entente for the loss of Russia. [They are also beginning] to realize the impossibility of continuing to transport so many troops, and so much war material and provisions across the ocean. America can only continue the war with any prospect of success if she is willing to prepare herself to fight for years. Even the most fanatic warmonger has no desire to do this. The whole nation is said to be depressed by the situation and Wilson to be under increasing pressure as a result of the general mood to find a way out. . . . There are many men in high government circles who know Germany very well and believe that America with her untrained troops never can defeat the veteran German Army.

Evidenzbureau 5784 1918/1919

Military Attaché in the Haag

Evb. 10976   20.4.1918

Recently America has had to consider the possibility that England will desert and make peace under terms which are not too unfavorable. On the other hand France is viewed as much more reliable as far as the continuation of the war is concerned. Since the conclusion of peace in Eastern Europe, America, which naturally means Wilson, has been determined to carry on the war under all circumstances, even without England. In order to limit England's freedom of action she has for some time now made all food and supply shipments to France from where the portion destined for England is then sent on.

§   While the diplomats and reporters formed their opinions, the fighting went on. There were more and more Americans at the front, and there were more prisoners.

M. Kr. 1832
No. 14591   GHQSM   1.3.18

. . . Our patrols which pushed forward over the canal at La Fère and penetrated the enemy trenches at Chavignon brought back some English prisoners from La Fère and 10 Americans and some Frenchmen from Chavignon. . . .

M. Kr. 1832

No. 14611   GHQSM   2.3.18

. . . 12 Americans were captured at Seicheprey between the Meuse and the Mosel; the latter are supposed to have suffered particularly heavy losses as a result of our deep forward thrust.

§   The war went on and on.

Personal Affairs of the Württemberg War Minister, Vol. 98

No. 11358   1.4.18

. . . Army Sector C:[28] Renewed artillery barrage near Saint-

---

[28] The designations A.A.A., A.A.B., and A.A.C. (Armee Abteilung, i.e. Section, or Sector) refer to the subdivisions of the Army Group under Duke

Mihiel. There is heavy traffic on the road leading north from Toul.
Because American radio messages have recently been overheard in
this area, it seems that the traffic is connected with the employment
of American troops.

M. Kr. 1832

No. 14961   GHQSM   4.4.18

... Army Sector C: An American was captured in a patrol action,
which confirmed the presence of the Fourth American Division in
the trenches.

M. Kr. 1832

No. 15091   GHQSM   14.4.18

... North of Saint-Mihiel a patrol returned with 23 Americans
and a light machine gun.... Our batteries bombarded the enemy
rear areas and battery emplacements . . . with gas.

M. Kr. 1832

No. 15451   GHQSM   11.5.18

... We inflicted heavy losses upon the Americans at Apremont
and in the Forest of Parroy with heavy mortar fire.

M. Kr. 1832

No. 15371   GHQSM   6.5.18

... Army Sector A ... Southwest of Blamont an American was
taken prisoner.

Albert of Württemberg which occupied the trenches from the area around
Verdun to the Swiss border. This portion of the Western Front was subdi-
vided from north to south in the following way: Army Sector C occupied the
ground north of Metz and was responsible for the *Michel-Stellung*. To the
south the 19th Army separated it from Sectors A and B. Army Sector C was
placed under the command of General von Gallwitz at the beginning of 1918
and formed part of Army Group Gallwitz until the end of the war.

M. Kr. 1832

No. 15391   GHQSM   7.5.18

. . . Army Sector C . . . In the southern part of the Front at Lienay two Americans were captured. . . .

M. Kr. 1832

No. 15411   GHQSM   8.5.18

. . . Army Sector C . . . Limited fighting. An American plane was shot down.

M. Kr. 1832

No. 15441   GHQSM   10.5.18

. . . Army Sector C . . . An enemy thrust at Seicheprey left behind one officer, two Americans, and two machine guns.

M. Kr. 1832

No. 15491   GHQSM   15.5.18

. . . 7th Army . . . In front of the left wing some men in mud-colored uniforms with flat steel helmets were recognized; it appears that either Englishmen or Americans have been put in the line.

M. Kr. 1832

No. 15631   GHQSM   28.5.18

. . . At Montdidier several Americans were captured and two machine guns taken as booty.

CHAPTER VI

The Grand Tour Draws to an End

§   In June the American First and Second divisions serving under General Mangin had helped to stop the German offensive on the Marne, and then later the Americans had distinguished themselves by taking Belleau Wood and Vaux on either side of the Château-Thierry salient, which marked the final boundary of the German advance.[1] Pershing had good arguments in his favor, and by August he had his own army.

The Americans proceeded to play their part in what the British like to call the 100 Days' Battle when "all the world" moved to attack the Germans. Two names loom large in the story of the American participation in these final struggles. They are Saint-Mihiel and the Meuse-Argonne. The German army that opposed them was not the army which had moved to the assault in March. Since then this army had suffered more than a million casualties. Many of the best men were gone and "Flanders fever" (Spanish influenza) had taken its toll of the rest. Gerhard Ritter describes portions of the German line being held by small groups of officers manning machine guns. Ludendorff insisted that the ground won in the

---

[1] C. Falls, *The Great War* (New York: G. P. Putnam's, 1959), 346–47; B. H. Liddell Hart, *Through the Fog of War* (London: Faber and Faber, 1938), 326.

spring offensive be held, despite the wishes of the field commanders for an orderly retirement from the salients created
by the spring offensives.[2] The reluctance of the OHL to give
up the ground taken in the spring made the defense all the
more difficult and presented Ludendorff with the terrible
prospect that his overextended front would collapse.[3] Fortunately for the Germans it never did, even in the face of
masses of fresh American troops supported by endless squadrons of tanks. This was due in part to the inexperience of the
Americans and in part to the very effective German defense
in depth which forced the attacker to move through a series
of battle zones which were lightly held by mutually supporting strong points and machine gun nests before ever reaching
the main defense line, which itself was constructed for a
defense in depth.

The first big American "push" against the Germans was
carried out by the American First Army on September 12.
The object was to cut the Saint-Mihiel salient by closing its
neck. The Germans were in the process of evacuating the
entire position when the six American divisions struck its
sides. Rapid progress was made, and the Germans were
pushed back in confusion to the Michel position (which was
not yet complete), but Pershing kept too tight a rein on his
divisions and the bulk of the Germans slipped away before
the sack was closed. Three quarters of the German casualties
in this battle were prisoners.[4] Later evidence indicates the
Americans might have pushed further, but they did not.[5]

Two weeks later, west of Verdun, an even larger force of
nine divisions moved against the Meuse-Argonne position.

---

[2] Brigadier-General Sir James E. Edmonds, *A Short History of World War I* (Oxford: Oxford University Press, 1951), 336; Gerhard Ritter, *Staatskunst und Kriegshandwerk,* 4 vols. (München: Verlag R. Oldenbourg, 1968), IV, 417.

[3] Ritter, IV, 417.

[4] Peter Graf Kielmansegg, *Deutschland und der Erste Weltkrieg* (Frank-furt: Akademische Verlagsgesellschaft Athenaion, 1968), 659.

[5] Liddell Hart, 229–331.

The Americans faced a river, the Meuse, a forest, the Argonne, and in the center a ridge, the Montfauçon ridge. The nine divisions engaged were green and, despite terrible losses and an advance, the offensive was not a success.[6] The French in particular were disgusted with Pershing. After another American attack on October 14 failed, there was talk that Foch would have Pershing removed.[7] As a result of the American failure the British General Staff had concluded in an appraisal of the German request for an armistice a few days before that it would probably take until 1920 for the Americans to develop the capacity to crush the Germans.

The American Army is disorganized, ill-equipped, and ill-trained. It has suffered heavily through ignorance of modern war conditions and it must be at least a year before it becomes a serious force.[8]

These pessimistic conclusions were the result of a careful appraisal of the Meuse-Argonne offensive that revealed lack of coordination at all levels. Roads to the front were blocked with transportation units, all racing forward without any order. Supplies were looted by passing troops and reinforcements, and food and ammunition could not get through. Army Headquarters appeared unable to control the situation.

. . . American divisions employed in large blocks under their own command, suffer wastage out of all proportion to results achieved, and generally do not pull more than a small fraction of their weight.

The report blamed Pershing for demanding an independent American command long before the Americans were ready for it.[9] When the offensive was resumed on November 1 the Americans moved forward and finally on November 7 cut the key Sedan railway which was the whole point of the

---

[6] Liddell Hart, 331–333.

[7] W.O. 106/528/8701, Letter from Lieutenant General Du Cane at Foch's Headquarters, 25.10.18.

[8] W.O. 158/20, General Staff Notes 18/10/1918.

[9] W.O. 106/528/8701, Notes on American Offensive Operations.

Meuse-Argonne offensive. The British report on this phase of the operation was much more optimistic, but then the war was over.[10]

News of the growing American presence began to fill the German reports in July 1918. The following report was sent from GHQSM to Munich.

M. Kr. 1775

Report 16

No. 13160   Foreign Armies Section   12 July 1918

1. Troops in Europe
[22 divisions were reported; 11 being employed at the front.] Indications that American troops are serving in French or British units are becoming more frequent. So far it has involved only assignment for training at the front or further instruction behind the front. Now it is also possible that complete American battalions or brigades will be incorporated into French and English divisions for a longer period of time. [Secretary Baker's claim that as of July 1 a million men have been sent to France was reported along with the monthly figures, which he released. They were: January, 46,776; February, 48,227; March, 83,811; April, 117,212; May, 244,345; June, 276,372.]
The transportation figures could be correct. However they refer not only to soldiers but to all the Americans who have been sent across. The American government itself admits that of the one million, only about 60% (600,000 men) are combat troops. The term "combat troops" is elastic. The supply trains, medical and engineering troops of the operational area are doubtless included within it. The ration strength of a division including corps troops, is, according to a captured order, 25,000 men. . . . The number of those who are not considered combat troops, 400,000 men, is very significant. Besides technical and labor formations, factory and dock laborers, the administrative personnel for the camps and harbors may also be included in these figures. The large number can be explained by the

---

[10] Liddell Hart, 333; W.O. 106/499A, 16 Nov. 1918.

size of the American effort in the harbors, supply bases, railways and factories.

The chief ports of embarkation in the United States have been identified through statements made by prisoners. They are New York and Philadelphia.

The debarkation of the troops has so far taken place in Bordeaux, Saint-Nazaire, Brest and Le Havre [the latter harbor for the troops arriving via Liverpool and Southampton]. . . .

§   Growing concern about the loss of manpower caused by the war was common to both sides. A meeting of the Imperial War Cabinet on July 18, 1918, devoted its attention to the problem. There had been complaints from the Dominions and the United States that Britain was not pulling her weight. The Cabinet were anxious to find a way to counter such rumors.

Sir Robert Borden advised the British government to follow the Canadian example and publish their casualty lists, but his suggestion was not followed. There was real concern that if the figures of over 3,000,000 casualties were made public, the next German peace overture would find support among the British voters.[11]

The way the same problem was faced by the German federal states is revealed in the following report made after the war.

Colonel Holland, who took General von Graevenitz's place as military plenipotentiary at GHQSM in July 1918, made his final report to the Württemberg War Minister, Freiherr Carl von Weizäcker, on April 6, 1919.[12]

---

[11] W.O. 106/475, Extract of the 25th meeting of the Imperial War Cabinet.

[12] Like the Bavarian representatives, the Württemberg military plenipotentiary and deputy plenipotentiary changed during the course of the year. Lieutenant General Friedrich Gustav von Graevenitz sent the bulk of the reports from GHQ during the first half of 1918. He was replaced by Colonel Holland in July 1918. Major General von Faber du Faur remained deputy military plenipotentiary in Berlin. General Karl von Knoerzer was von Graevenitz's predecessor. All reports went to Freiherr Carl von Weizäcker, Minister of War and External Affairs.

Personal Affairs of the Württemberg War Minister, Vol. 245.

Final Report of the Military Plenipotentiary at
General Headquarters, April 1919

BERLIN-WILMERSDORF, 6.IV.1919

[Holland explained that he received his instructions from the War Minister in Stuttgart on July 16.] He informed me that, in view of the particularly heavy losses suffered by Württemberg troops throughout the war and especially in the course of the 1918 spring offensive it was of utmost importance to conserve them wherever possible. [Lieutenant General von Graevenitz had already initiated such steps with good results. However, Holland reported with regret that the failure of the last German offensive on July 15 and the beginning of the Allied counteroffensive on July 18 made his task far more difficult.] Then on the 18th the successful Allied counteroffensive against the right flank of the Marne [salient], which resulted in unusually heavy German casualties, began. [All attempts to obtain relief for the 24th Division failed because it held a vital position. The 27th Division, which was resting in the IInd Army Area, a quiet sector of the trenches, was caught in the August 8 offensive. The thrust against the IInd Army made it impossible to relieve the 243rd Division, or any of the other Württemberg divisions at the front.] In the defensive battle a large number of divisions gave way, because the replacements which they had received after the spring offensive had been stirred up against the authority of their officers by the agitation that was being systematically carried on at home and being brought to the front lines. On the whole they were not merely war weary but were in fact openly hostile toward fighting at all. [Holland described the greeting given to the 243rd Division, as it was being brought up to the front, by Prussian units returning from the trenches.] Here come the damned Swabians again, who always want to hold out. Turn around now and come along with us. [The Colonel then explained that the large number of prisoners taken by the enemy at this time was due to the collapse of such divisions which left holes in the German line. The Allies were able to exploit these gaps and to surround troops which were still fighting. Unreliable divisions were a great danger and had to be taken out of the line as soon as possible. These developments caused the rapid exhaustion of existing reserves and made it necessary to put sound troops back into the trenches, regardless of the losses which they had already suffered.] The four Württemberg divisions which have already been mentioned belonged to those [units] which without exception continued to fight magnificently.

In fact it was just these four excellent divisions, as well as many proven Prussian units, which had to pay for the pernicious agitation at home with prolonged duty in particularly severe fighting and with heavy and ever-increasing sacrifices in blood. [When rumors that Württemberg troops were being thrown into the battle more frequently than Prussian units reached the War Minister, he demanded fair treatment and relief for his troops. The commanders of the divisions in question replied to him that, despite the complaints of the troops, Württemberg's soldiers were not being abused. Reliable Prussian divisions were being kept in the line just as long. On the 6th of September Colonel Holland had an interview with Ludendorff and asked him to spare the Württemberg divisions further heavy losses. Ludendorff agreed, as far as the situation allowed. At Colonel Holland's suggestion on September 7 General von Schippert, commander of the 243rd Division, along with one of his regimental commanders, lectured to the staff officers at GHQ on conditions at the front.][13] The serious situation [at the front] made necessary the use of our troops in October. Therefore they could no longer be conserved. . . .

§   Just what these losses meant is brought out in the report Holland delivered from GHQ on August 8, 1918, the "Black Day" of the German Army, about the 54th Reserve Division.[14] The result of the losses in the Marne offensive and in

---

[13] The Bavarian military plenipoteniary was delighted with this development and hoped the statements of the two officers, especially that of the regimental commander, would bring home to the High Command the seriousness of the situation at the front.

[14] *Kriegsministerium. Abteilung für allgemeine Armee- und persönliche Angelegenheiten: Kriegsakten betreff: 54 Reserve Division, Januar 1917 bis Nov. 1918;* Item 18 GHQ, 8 August 1918.

meeting the French counteroffensive was that the battalions of the 54th Reserve Division now numbered about 300 men apiece rather than 600. Holland noted that the rate of loss was about the same in Bavarian, Saxon, and Prussian units that had been similarly engaged. Prussian and Bavarian divisions that had suffered such losses had already been broken up and, Holland said, there was no reason not to do the same with the 54th Reserve Division.

A view of the Americans less than two weeks before the failure of the last German offensive is given in the following report.

M. Kr. 1775 Special

Chief of the General Staff of the Field Army, Foreign Armies Section

Report No. 15

No. 12522   GHQSM   2.7.1918

[The report began by stating that before America's entry into the war there were 1,500 Americans in the Allied armies. They included pilots, supply troops, and medical units. The first American troops arrived at the end of July 1917 and by the fall of 1917 there were 40,000 men in Europe. At the end of October one American division went into action. The Americans had agreed to send between 450,000 and 500,000 men by the end of April 1917. Two additional divisions had reached Europe by the end of 1917. The Foreign Armies Section issued its *The Military Situation of the Entente in the Winter of 1917/1918* (No. 6730 a, December 1917), which estimated that by the end of the spring of 1918 the Americans would have 15 divisions in France. At the time of the German offensive the Allies were disappointed because the expected number of American troops had not arrived. However since April the transport of American troops had greatly increased, there were now between 7 and 8 divisions at the front and another 9 or 10 already in Europe; 26 were undergoing training in the United States.] There can be no doubt about the American intention to commit their entire strength to the war. . . . The possibility of transporting 26 divisions this year and of solving the entire supply problem for the American Army depends upon the availability of shipping space. In view of the American achievements in transportation during recent months they may well solve the problem and carry out the task. . . . A temporary increase in troop shipments is possible if for a while after the harvest in Europe, the import of food can be suspended. Our submarines have so far had no effect upon the transport of troops.

Considering its small experience of war and defective training the combat value of the American division can in general be described as good. In defense even the most recently arrived troops represent an opponent worthy of respect. The American soldier shows himself to be brave, strong, and skillful. Losses are not avoided. However their leadership is not yet all that good. With the appearance of Americans in larger independent units, French guidance and help, at least at first, are essential.

In the assessment of the combat worth of the Americans, the fact that the troops which have arrived to date are an elite must be taken into account. It remains to be seen if the divisions which are still to come will be of the same value. The recently identified 77th Division showed distinctly bad morale and an inferior spirit. Its poor performance can be attributed to faulty training and to its being employed too early. Indifference to the war aims is striking even among the best American troops. They do not know for what they are fighting. Consequently after longer service at the front a general decline in the desire to fight is quite possible.

Personal Affairs of the Württemberg War Minister, Vol. 102

No. 12984   GHQSM   5.8.18

. . . Army Sector B. . . . At Altkirch four Americans, who belong to the 29th American Division which was not believed to be in France, were taken prisoner. . . . Including this one the number of American divisions in France amounts to 28.

§   The Foreign Armies Section of the General Staff issued the following report, which was forwarded to Munich.

M. Kr. 1775

Report 16

No. 15660   GHQSM   23.8.1918

1. Troops in Europe. . . .

According to the statement of the Chief of the General Staff, the United States is in a position to send 250,000 men per month to France until the beginning of winter. America intends to have an army of 2,300,000 men in France on 1.1.19 and to increase the size of this army by the time of Foch's great offensive in the year 1919 to three million men. . . .

§   As Germany's situation worsened, one thoughtful critic of her military policy, Professor Hans Delbrück, published a long article that considered Germany's relations with the rest of the world.

SINCERE DESIRE FOR PEACE
SUBMARINE WARFARE AND AMERICA
(from *Krieg und Politik*)[15]

18. August 1918

The German people entered the World War in the knowledge that they were fighting an honorable and just, defensive war. We felt that we had been attacked from all sides. We ourselves did not desire war and were fully convinced that the Emperor and his Chancellor, Mr. von Bethmann Hollweg, were also completely peacefully inclined and sought nothing more than to maintain for the German Empire

---

[15] Hans Delbrück, *Krieg und Politik,* 3 vols. (Berlin: Verlag von Georg Stilke, 1919), III, 137–152.

and the German people an honorable place as an equal among the great nations of the world. Although it has come to the most terrible slaughter, we will always be able to remain convinced that the guilt lies with our opponents.

However, as far as their behavior during the war itself is concerned the German people do not stand nearly as well. The heroism of the struggle and the unanimity and determination of the political parties in the struggle against the foe is beyond praise. But we must carefully consider the situation politically. The expansion and prolongation of the war is, despite our repeated offers of peace, indeed to no small degree our responsibility. Whence do our opponents find the amazing strength for the enormous tenacity of their will to destroy us? Entirely from the hate which they nourish against us? Out of the envy of our flourishing wealth which fills them? Merely from rage caused by a war psychosis? Anyone who follows the press of any of the enemy countries finds again and again the observation that: if Germany is not subdued, the world can no longer enjoy peace; the future of all nations stands in the balance and is threatened by us; the wounds and losses of this war will be quickly healed and the warlike spirit of our people will again assert itself and lead to new adventures; the great nations fight not only for themselves but at the same time for the freedom of all smaller nations and for the freedom of the world.

These views are also championed with particular eloquence by the former American ambassador, Gerard, in the memoirs of his stay in Berlin, which are filled with deep hostility towards us and are quite unreliable but brilliantly written. He has prophesied that once Germany has dominated Europe, she will then threaten the United States. This would not necessarily be a direct threat but would result from the conquest of some area or other in Central or South America to which it is not much more difficult to transport troops from Germany than from the United States. In the American Senate it has even been imagined that Germany would take control of all of Russia and then attack the United States through Siberia. Frightened by such ideas, the nations grit their teeth and form themselves row on row and make sacrifice upon sacrifice in order, as Lloyd George has expressed it, not to burden the next generation with a more terrible conflict by ending the present war too hastily. It would be both too easy and also very irresponsible to seek to dismiss this view as the purest hypocrisy. It is really present and sincerely believed by endless numbers of people and is the actual source of strength for the efforts of the Western nations.

Could such a feeling, which fills the whole world, have arisen if from the very beginning of the war Germany, despite her military success, had confined herself to waging a defensive war and had sought no increase of her power? If we had always insisted upon being involved in the colonialism of the Great Powers as was fitting for us, but had demanded nothing more in Europe?

Let us go back somewhat further to the time before the war. Surely we did not desire war, but nevertheless we must confess that we had in Germany a movement which aroused the suspicion of other nations and was too little noticed by our own public opinion, and certainly not nearly sharply enough rejected by it. We knew our own people so little that the majority saw in Revolutionary Social Democracy the future danger which threatened us. The *Prussian Yearbooks* bear witness that long before the war I have said the Pan-Germans were much more dangerous than the Social Democrats, because they could involve us in a war which could otherwise be avoided. The ambassador in Washington, Count Bernstorff, has severely criticised the provocations of the Pan-Germans and, once when Mr. von Heydebrand used exuberant chauvinistic expressions, the Imperial Chancellor, von Bethmann Hollweg, refuted him mercilessly. There has been no lack of resistance but the war first showed us how greatly Pan-German agitation had damaged us and how much each exaggerated statement had been utilized by the chauvinistic parties of the enemy who are of the same mind. Together with this the unwise Naval policy of Admiral von Tirpitz, who instead of submarines built dreadnoughts, which now cannot at all prevent the blockade of the North Sea, and which aroused the suspicions of the English to the point of hatred, has brought about a most calamitous result. The idea that Germany strives for world hegemony which today is believed by all nations is only a further development of the suspicions which were already present before the war. Instead of doing everything to remove these suspicions we have done all too much to strengthen them.

The theory has been advanced that when peace is concluded, Germany must increase her power to such an extent that no one will again dare to attack her. But no consideration has been given to the fact that a power which can no longer be attacked by anyone, even a coalition, is itself in a position to attack others and is a threat to these others who will employ every means to defend themselves. Germany has been fascinated by this idea which has again and again been proclaimed anew in the Reichstag. The leader of the Center, Mr. Spahn, demanded that we take political, military and economic control of Belgium, as did Mr. Müller-Meiningen of the Liberals. In the spring of 1915 the six great economic associations presented their petitions in which they demanded not only Belgium and thousands of square miles from France and Poland but also insisted that all the large landowners, or indeed the entire population, should be removed from the regions which were to be obtained in order to control the territory better, or to make it German. A petition of more than a thousand notables led by several professors supported these demands. Today it is almost painful to remember these proceedings. However because the greater part of the German people still supports the leaders who formerly infatuated them with such mad ideas, the attempt must be made, . . . to bring them to reason. These are the same circles who with confident mien promised us that unlimited submarine warfare would bring the English to their knees within six months. These are the same elements who swore to us that America was only bluffing, that she was not in a position to raise an army, and that if she should raise an army, she would not be able to send it to Europe. It is these very circles who on account of his moderation have persecuted the Chancellor, von Bethmann Hollweg, with the most vicious slander. This is the same crowd which has come together in the Fatherland Party and torn apart the unity of the German people. These are the very people who, when the majority of the German people's representatives all too tardily made way for political prudence, rewarded them for this with insults.

As that petition which demanded the acquisition of vast regions in East and West went around for signatures, it was said that these demands did not need to be fulfilled completely. One could be satisfied with less. Reference was simply made to our enemy's will to destroy us and to the enormous demands which could be heard from the other side.

But how have these English and French demands influenced us? One can say that they have become our best allies in strengthening our people's unshakable determination to hold out. On the basis of this experience one can judge how the German plans have driven our enemies to exert their strength to the fullest. The German patriots did not take this into account when they claimed that it does no harm to demand a little bit too much and that it gave no offense to sign unfortunate petitions. If our violation of Belgian neutrality which we could excuse in terms of self-defense was already taken ill enough by the other side, then what has followed it appears to prove fully German malignance. Today the German people must pay the penalty for the results. The mistrust of the world once aroused by these and similar actions is not so easily put to rest again and in this mistrust of our pursuit of power lies one of the greatest hindrances to peace.

One can cite the fact that the German government never agreed with these fanatics for conquest, that on the contrary the Imperial Chancellor, von Bethmann Hollweg, had to submit to the most furious attacks because he rejected the plans of such people, and that his successor continued his policy without any basic change. But that is not enough. In my observations of the preceding month I have said here that Mr. von Bethmann Hollweg has used the expression "a pledge of security" with respect to Belgium and by so doing has announced that we do not intend to retain it. This was not entirely correct. To be sure Mr. von Bethmann Hollweg was the first to use the word "pledge of security" in the Reichstag (9th December 1915) with reference not to Belgium but to other areas which the sword has put under our authority. It was only during the debate that the word was also applied to Belgium by the Social Democratic member, Landsberg, and as a result of this became generally accepted.

But the difference is not great, although Mr. von Bethmann Hollweg has given in so far to the annexationist tendency that he has demanded "substantial" guarantees Belgium cannot be used as an area of concentration for our foes in a future war; and such "substantial guarantees" can easily be interpreted as a kind of sovereignty. Mr. von Bethmann Hollweg himself can be defended against the charge that he wished to reduce Belgium to the status of a German vassal state by means of "guarantees." He has completely denied what Gerard says about this in his book and it is also refuted by all of his statements. He has expressly and repeatedly (19 August 1915, 9 December 1915) emphasized the defensive character of the war and has defended us against the charge that we threatened small nations: "We do not wage this war which was forced upon us to subdue foreign nations but rather to defend our lives and freedom."

Enemy suspicion was however too great and too strong to be overcome by such a slogan, which is quite vague. Regardless of whether Mr. von Bethmann Hollweg has made these demands concerning Belgium because he himself considers "substantial guarantees" necessary or whether he has done so out of consideration for our chauvinists at home, they remain a spur and a stimulus to our enemies' will to fight. For they want to protect themselves not only from the aims of our present government but also from the possible evil intention of a future government for which they believe they can see the tendency and potential in our national life. They refer to Prussian militarism linked with the ideology of Pan-Germanism.

.   .   .   .   .

Wherever we look we can see that neither the German government nor the German people have done everything which was advisable and within their power to vouch for the honesty of their desire for peace and respect for the rights of smaller nations. On the contrary we have done all too much to strengthen the leaders of the war parties on the other side, Mr. Lloyd George and Mr. Clemenceau, and have put evidence in their hands that the Germans are possessed of a spirit which threatens the freedom of other nations.

.   .   .   .   .

Nothing revenges itself more in politics than the underestimation of the enemy and the overestimation of one's own strength. The soldier can and should think differently; he must believe that he is able to take on the whole world. Nevertheless strategy consists not merely in the advance, for timely retreats have been accepted in the history of the world, and also in this war as masterpieces of the art of generalship. In politics a cautious estimate of the balance of strength in the world is the real secret of lasting success.

.   .   .   .   .

In this connection the declaration of unrestricted submarine warfare as of 1 February, 1917, about which new theories requiring discussion have recently seen the light of day, is to be evaluated. First of all it must be stated that those who at the time recommended this move to us were so incorrect in their predictions that one may be permitted to describe them as politically incompetent. We were most firmly promised that within a few months England would be so damaged that she would have to beg us for peace. The chief spokesman for this agitation, Count Reventlow, claims in the *Deutschen Tageszeitung* that he has never presented a fixed time limit. This claim stands in sharp contrast to the facts. Count Reventlow was however more cautious than Grand Admiral von Tirpitz because he did not name a specific number of months. He not only promised the "speedy" reduction of England (*Deutsche Tageszeitung* of December, 1916) but also always maintained that the admirals who recommended "unrestricted" submarine warfare were in every way competent to make a judgment. When I protested that the admirals certainly were competent on the naval-technical side of the question but that an economic aspect which required an entirely different knowledge was also involved, Count Reventlow answered me contemptuously that the admirals were able to judge these things as well. We now know what to think of this judgment. The same is true of the judgment concerning America's entry into the war. Only great political ignorance could have expounded or attributed to our governing circles the thoughts that the entry of this enormous state meant nothing militarily, or that, as this same Count Reventlow proclaimed with particular pleasure, America's participation would be more advantageous to us than her hostile neutrality.

.   .   .   .   .

Public opinion in Germany would have never been won for "unrestricted" submarine warfare if they had been told from the beginning that this means would not after a year and a half have brought us peace but instead that we would have drawn the United States as an additional foe down upon our necks; and these gentlemen who led us into such a basic error concerning these matters remain responsible for it. . . .

Ambassador Gerard's book gives us in its malevolence a very good view of the American attitude and feeling. The book contradicts itself. In one place there is a careful description of how the ambassador despite all kinds of conflicts made every effort to maintain peace between the two powers until Germany's declaration of 1 February 1917 destroyed everything and made the war unavoidable. According to this America could have continued to remain neutral.

On the other hand it is equally thoroughly demonstrated that the militaristic-tyrannical spirit of the Prussian-German State made peaceful co-existence impossible and compelled America for the sake of her own freedom and that of the world to draw the sword. . . .

The world today cannot find the peace which it seeks, because parties exist on both sides which are so filled with suspicion that they see their own future security guaranteed only by the complete destruction of the enemy. The difference is that in England and France these same parties rule; but not in Germany, though such elements are so strong that so far they have hindered the development of a proper policy. Here as there, though in different degrees, it is necessary to make clear to the public that the so-called assurances for which it is believed one must fight, are in truth not essential. In Germany a good deal in this respect has already taken place. Since Hertling's explanation about Belgium has been issued, talk concerning the Flanders Coast is as good as silenced. To be sure the "Fatherland Party" has not yet disbanded itself but it is hardly heard from anymore. If the government would finally take heart and declare open war upon the Pan-Germans and rally all the elements who sincerely support the idea of a League for World Peace and wish to work for it insofar as it can be realized, then a great deal would be won. . . .

The best way to prove to the world that those who rule Germany have finally and irrevocably shown the door to efforts of the Pan-Germans would be for the government to gather together all those prewar Pan-German provocations and demonstrate from enemy propaganda literature how much this conduct has damaged us and contributed to causing the catastrophe of war. By such an act they would give to the German people and to the world convincing evidence that they want nothing to do with such depravity and that they are animated by a true and honest desire for peace. The world demands and has a right to demand that the German people give it surety that the Pan-German spirit, the spirit of arrogance, of force, of hostility to education and of paganism is not the German spirit. If one says that in other nations chauvinism and jingoism have produced much more poisonous flowers than our Pan-Germanism, and that consequently we have to demand from our foes the same kind of guarantees, or even greater ones, than they require of us, one can

answer this by saying that the comparison does not fit. Chauvinism
on the other side, particularly in France, was the governing power
and we have created a guarantee against the repetition of its attacks
in that we have shown that they can achieve nothing against us. But
Pan-Germanism was always only a sect among us, a group of fanatics without real influence, until the war psychosis brought it real
importance. Superstition and suspicion have increased its importance to the point of frightfulness in the eyes of our foes. It is this
misinterpretation which in the interest of peace we must combat and
where possible remove. This is not only diplomatic wisdom but also
a moral obligation because Pan-Germanism has won a place among
us which has morally tainted our national character.

§   The following excerpts give a graphic account of the last
months of war as seen from various perspectives.

The reports of the Württemberg and Bavarian military
plenipotentiaries give the story of the Americans from Belleau Woods and Château-Thierry to Saint-Mihiel and the
battles on the Meuse and in the Argonne during the fall. The
reports are taken from Volumes 100 and 101, IVa 55, of the
Personal Affairs of the Württemberg War Minister and from
the M. Kr. 1832 series of the reports to the Bavarian War
Minister.

The War Diary of General Theodore Freiherr von Wat-
ter's XIII Army Corps, which in the last months of the war
was part of the Seventh Army, gives a vivid account of the
Allied offensive of July 18, 1918. The story it tells fills in
some of the background for the account given by the reports
from Supreme Headquarters. The following excerpt is taken
from the copy of the Diary which is at the Heeresarchiv in
Stuttgart.

Vol. 100

No. 12196   GHQSM   5 June 1918

The body of one dead American was discovered in the Belleau
Woods region held by Group Conta.

M. Kr. 1832

No. 15581   GHQSM   2.6.18

...Army Sector B. West of Thann enemy reliefs appear to be underway. Americans have been put into the line on our extreme left wing.... Enemy resistance has become so strong that further advances are no longer possible without too great a sacrifice. Therefore the army will for the present cease its advance, in order to resume the offensive after a thorough preparation for it. Consequently there has been no change in our position.... Group Conta: ... In Château-Thierry enemy resistance has been broken.... Today heavy enemy reinforcements are again being brought up.

M. Kr. 1832

No. 15721   GHQSM   6.6.18

...On the right wing at Belleau Wood and Bussiares there has been heavy enemy harassing fire. Since early today an enemy attack has been underway in this area, which is to be repulsed by a counterattack....

M. Kr. 1832

No. 15731   GHQSM   7.6.18

An American-English-French attack upon the right wing of Conta (Group Conta) towards Veuilly and Bussiares was initially successful; our lines were forced back as far as Bussiares. Our counterattack won back all of the lost ground. What was involved here was a limited operation of a larger sort. A further enemy attack against Torcy and Belleau collapsed in the face of our defensive fire.

M. Kr. 1832

No. 15741   GHQSM   8.6.18

...Contrary to the Eifel tower report, Hill 204 west of Château-Thierry is firmly in our hands; several Americans were taken prisoner there. An American and a French division, as well as parts of two other French divisions, have taken part in the enemy advance towards the Clignon stream....

174 OVER THERE

Vol. 100

No. 12230   GHQSM   8 June 1918

... [Belleau Wood south of the Torcy-Belleau road]. ... The enemy attack against the latter area failed with heavy losses. The Eifel news report which claimed that we had lost Hill 204 west of Château-Thierry is, according to our troops, incorrect. One English, one American and parts of two French divisions seem to have taken part in the assault. An additional French division is said to have been ready in the third line to exploit a possible success. ...

M. Kr. 1832

No. 15751   GHQSM   9.6.18

... Americans have been employed on the left wing of the 19th Army ... Main Battlefield ... Group Conta: An enemy attack against Belleau Wood was driven back with heavy losses; 12 Americans were captured. The situation on the Marne is unchanged. ...

M. Kr. 1832

No. 15769   GHQSM   10.6.18

... (right flank of Group Conta) ... West of Château-Thierry elements of the American 3rd Division were identified during the fighting. This division arrived fresh and practically untrained at the end of April. ...

Vol. 100

No. 12301   GHQSM   12 June 1918

(Shown to His Majesty on 15.6)

... 7th Army ... Northwest of Château-Thierry heavy enemy attacks against Belleau Wood failed. ...

M. Kr. 1832

No. 15791   GHQSM   12.6.18

... 4th Army ... According to statements made by prisoners, Americans have arrived in the trenches for training at Meteren. The 7th Army again repulsed with heavy losses for the enemy repeated, powerful attacks against Belleau Wood and west of Château-Thierry.

Vol. 100

No. 12310   GHQSM   13 June 1918

... 7th Army ... After a heavy preparatory barrage, American troops penetrated Belleau Wood in the Group Conta area. Their attempt to break through beyond the Wood failed. It is now under our concentrated gas and shrapnel fire. Apparently the Boureschés village was also attacked. There is no news about it.

M. Kr. 1832

No. 15801   GHQSM   13.6.18

... In the Group Conta area the Americans, after a concentrated artillery preparation, succeeded in taking possession of Belleau Wood. For some time now Belleau Wood has been under our gas and shrapnel fire. An enemy attack against Boureschés seems to have been successful. ...

M. Kr. 1832

No. 15811   GHQSM   14.6.18

... 7th Army ... Heavy assaults ... upon Hill 204 West of Château-Thierry, where the Americans attacked, were repulsed. On the 1st Army Front there was moderate artillery activity which began southeast of Rheims. An enemy observer was clearly identified on the Cathedral and thereafter we shelled the Cathedral.

M. Kr. 1832

No. 15821   GHQSM   15.6.18

... As a result of our bombardment of Belleau Wood large enemy formations have fled from the forest southward. ...

§   The next day two more American divisions were reported between the Aisne and the Oise. (15831, 16.6.18)

M. Kr. 1832

No. 15841   GHQSM   17.6.18

... Army Sector C: Our attack at Richecourt and Xivray inflicted painful losses upon the Americans in the trenches there and won some ground from them. . . .

M. Kr. 1832

No. 15871   GHQSM   20.6.18

... Army Sector C: ... [an attack on the Southern Front against Seicheprey] ... We penetrated deep into the American position, whose garrison defended themselves stubbornly.

Vol. 100

No. 12417   GHQSM   21 June 1918

... Northwest of Château-Thierry American troops sought to surprise our trench garrisons without any artillery preparation. The enemy was caught by our artillery and shot down. Pursuing patrols discovered 50 dead in a small area.

M. Kr. 1832

No. 15881   GHQSM   21.6.18

... 7th Army ... West of Château-Thierry Americans in dense masses attacked without any kind of artillery preparation. The attack was met by our artillery fire and shot to pieces.

Vol. 100

No. 12506   GHQSM   26 June 1918

... 7th Army ... Northwest of Château-Thierry an enemy attack which attempted to break through and out of the forest failed. . . . The fighting reported in the Belleau area has turned out to be very bitter. The enemy has succeeded in capturing a small portion of our trenches.

M. Kr. 1832

No. 15961   GHQSM   27.6.18

... 7th Army ... The final reports about yesterday's attack at
Belleau reveal that the enemy succeeded, after very heavy fighting,
in establishing himself in one small sector of our perimeter.

Vol. 101 IVa 55

Secret

No. 12600   GHQSM   7 July 1918

... 7th Army ... Yesterday morning the enemy bombardment of
our position in the line Vaux — Hill 204 — Château-Thierry greatly
increased. A joint Franco-American attack followed in the afternoon. It was easily repulsed on the right flank, while between Hill
204 and the Marne heavy hand-to-hand fighting continued into the
night. The enemy gained only little ground and suffered heavy losses. Hill 204 remained in German hands. For this attack a division of
the XXI French Army Corps, which is known to be very good, was
put in between the two American divisions, already in position there.

M. Kr. 1832

No. 16121   GHQSM   10.7.18

[a counterattack west of Château-Thierry] ... brought us back
into possession of the portion of the trenches between Hill 204 and
the Marne which was lost on 6.7.18. . . .

§   War Diary of the XIII Army Corps.

                         HQ Ecuiry   12.7.18

... The impression that the enemy intends to launch a large scale
attack is strengthened by the fact that he has concentrated only
good, completely battle ready divisions on our front and that he has
apparently gathered strong reserves in the forested area behind his

front. Recently the activity of his artillery has also greatly increased. . . .

Vol. 101 IVa 55

No. 12741   GHQSM   18 July 1918

[Heavy artillery fire was reported from as far away as the region
around Château-Thierry.] . . . A heavy French attack seems to be in
preparation . . . [the following phrase was added in pen] according to
our report has begun.

§   War Diary of the XIII Army Corps.

                         HQ Ecuiry and then Acy   18.7.18

. . . At 5:30 AM the heaviest enemy drum fire commenced suddenly against the entire Corps Sector as well as the areas beyond it
to the north and the south. An attack by enemy infantry against the
entire front followed shortly afterwards.

Reports from the forward area could not at first be obtained,
because after a short time all connections with it were shot to pieces.
Vigorous enemy fire of heavier caliber fell upon villages in the rear
areas and the approach march routes. . . . The bulk of our artillery
fell into the hands of the enemy when their breakthrough simply
overran the trench and ready reserve battalions whose battle
strength was limited,[16] so that at first only a few batteries were
available to repulse the fierce enemy attacks.

In addition to the greatly reduced and exhausted infantry of the
trench divisions, two regiments of the 3rd Reserve Division were

---

[16] Along with their defense in depth the Germans had developed highly
effective specialized units to handle the threat of breakthroughs. These units
were kept near the front ready for action but, as a result of the spring
offensive, both these units and those which specialized in holding the defensive area against the initial attack had been dangerously weakened. This
excerpt from the XIII Corps War Diary reveals clearly the decline in
German battle strength.

thrown in. The weight of the enemy attack fell upon this thin line of infantry which at first was deprived of practically all artillery support but the foe, who again and again threw fresh forces, accompanied by innumerable tanks, into the battle, was able to gain ground only slowly. . . .

Around noon the enemy succeeded in advancing further at Chaudun and Vierzy, and in taking Blanzy. . . .

At 2:00 PM a Corps order was issued that all heavy baggage and unnecessary vehicles of the Corps were to be removed beyond the line Laffaux – Jouy north of the Aisne. . . .

At 5:00 PM Corps HQ was pulled back from Ecuiry to Acy. . . .

Towards evening the enemy attacked again in great strength and with numerous tanks at Chaudun, Vierzy and the Mauloy Wood. . . .

Vol. 101 IVa 55

No. 12752   **GHQSM**   19 July 1918

. . . 9th and 7th Army . . . The French have launched exceptionally violent attacks upon a front of 50 kilometers between the Aisne and the region of Château-Thierry. To our surprise they were able to penetrate our lines in several places and to extend the ground which they had won on both sides of their position. [The attack was finally halted and a new defense line formed.] Yesterday afternoon fresh and violent assaults on this line were repulsed. Today at 5:00 AM a heavy artillery barrage was resumed, followed at 5:20 by infantry attacks.

M. Kr. 1832
No. 16251   **GHQSM**   20.7.18

. . . [Group Conta and Schmettow of the Seventh Army reported.] . . . Between the Aisne and Château-Thierry there was heavy fighting yesterday morning and afternoon with . . . numerous enemy forces supported by tanks. As a result of the outstanding defense and the splendid behavior of our troops the heavy enemy blow was parried and for the most part failed. Our defense was carried out in depth and the losses of terrain bear no relation to the enemy forces employed and the heavy losses which the enemy has suffered. Considering these conditions we must accept loss of ground.

Vol. 101 IVa 55

No. 12760   GHQSM   20 July 1918

... 9th and 7th Army ... The battle continues. ... Between the Aisne and Château-Thierry the French pressed their attacks throughout the day. They repeatedly threw fresh divisions and numerous formations of tanks into the battle. Our defense in depth brought the attacks to a standstill with only small loss of ground. ...

According to orders and unnoticed by the enemy, our troops which had crossed over to the south bank of the Marne were withdrawn to the north bank. They destroyed the guns which they had captured and took all their material with them. The engineer and bridgetrain troops have played an outstanding part in the successful execution of this move. So far the enemy has not followed. North of the Marne there is no change in the situation.

M. Kr. 1832

No. 16261   GHQSM   21.7.18

... 7th Army ... North of the Aisne English and Americans attacked Fontenoy; for a while they succeeded in breaking into the place but our counterattacks brought Fontenoy completely into our hands again. ... Strong American attacks against Boureschés were repelled with numerous enemy casualties. Yesterday's attack also extended to the left wing of Group Schoeler up to Hill 204 southwest of Château-Thierry. Here all the attacks were completely repulsed. ...

§   A letter with no report number, written on July 22, 1918, to the Bavarian War Minister by General von Köberle, revealed the real seriousness of the situation. "As I have already said before, it is uncertain whether the Marne front can be held. In any case the blow planned in Flanders cannot be carried out. . . ."

Vol. 101 IVa 55

No. 12791   GHQSM   22 July 1918

. . . At Ancervilles Stormtroops penetrated the enemy position and inflicted considerable losses upon the enemy. They brought back to our own lines 19 living, as well as 15 dead Americans, including one officer. . . .

M. Kr. 1832

No. 16282   GHQSM   23.7.18

. . . 7th Army . . . At Armentières southeast of Oulchy we have withdrawn our line about .600 meters further east as far as the bank of the stream. For a while Epiéds was occupied by the enemy but it was regained from him in the counterattack and in the process 138 Americans were taken prisoner and 12 machine guns were taken as booty. . . . The Western Front of the 7th Army and the Right Wing of the 1st Army expect an enemy attack today. . . .

M. Kr. 1832

No. 16291   GHQSM   24.7.18

. . . Main Battle Front: Yesterday was a hard day of heavy fighting for the 7th Army which was finally decided in our favor with the heaviest enemy losses. . . .

M. Kr. 1832

No. 16301   GHQSM   25.7.18

. . . Intensive local attacks which resulted in heavy casualties for the enemy were directed primarily against the southern portion of the 7th Army [front]. They were held on our present line or a little bit behind it.. . . .

After all the enemy attacks against the present front between Chatelet Wood – Epiéds – Jaulgonne were turned back, it appeared necessary to shorten our line further, in order to retain freedom of action for future operations. By so doing our strength was conserved and the opportunity to employ our troops offensively again in the decisive place during the course of this year retained.

§   The German offensive was finished and the last phase of the war had begun. The British name for this stage of the war is the 100 Days' Battle. Give or take a few days, the name sums it up very well.

M. Kr. 1832

No. 16431   GHQSM   4.8.18

Main Battlefront: Available enemy reserves are presently estimated at: 23 French, 14 English and 19 American divisions. The enemy forces employed from 5.7–2.8 total 58 divisions, namely; 44 French, 8 American, 4 English and 2 Italian divisions. In addition 2 cavalry divisions were employed.

M. Kr. 1832

No. 16501   GHQSM   11.8.18

. . . 2nd and 18th Army: . . . Employing unprecedented masses of tanks and fresh infantry forces, the English and the French resumed their offensive from Ancre to the Oise yesterday. Our defense in depth proved itself magnificently. Although according to orders which have been found the employment of masses of tanks is supposed to be decisive for the further course of the war and, despite the assault by waves of enemy infantry immediately following them, the enemy achieved no noteworthy success or major breakthrough.

§   The next day in a report which informed the Bavarian authorities of fresh attacks upon the 18th Army front from the Bois de Loges to the left wing of the First Army on the Oise, the presence of yet other American troops was reported. "The presence of an American division was revealed by the capture of 150 Americans."[17]

The so-called Black Day of the German Army, August 8, 1918, was not reported in the usual way. No. 16541, 14.8.18 was a longhand-written report on the Allied success at Amiens. Von Köberle explained the Allied success as due to the inability of the Germans to employ their artillery against the tanks of the enemy because of the fog. However he did not underestimate the significance of what had happened upon that day.

M. Kr. 1832

No. 16581   GHQSM   18.8.18

... Army Sector A ... After they had set Provenchères on fire with their artillery barrage, the Americans attacked our trenches, and after rather severe fighting on our perimeter, they gained a foothold in the ruins of the village of Frapelle ... which was held by only a few outposts.

M. Kr. 1832

No. 16711   GHQSM   28.8.18

... 7th Army A: A heavy American attack on both sides of the St. Thibaut-Bazoches road was repulsed, our own counterthrust put us in possession of Fismette. 250 Americans were captured.

M. Kr. 1832

No. 16901   GHQSM   13.9.18

... On the western portion of the front it was primarily the

---

[17] M. Kr. 1832, No. 16511, 12.8.18.

French who attacked, on the southern sector it was the Americans. After a four hour artillery preparation the latter attacked with a great many tanks. The withdrawal movement from our present trenches was only markedly disturbed by the attack on the southern front.

§   A long letter from von Köberle dated September 14, 1918, explained to the Bavarian Minister of War why so much material had been lost in the retreat from Saint-Mihiel. The loss of an entire battery of trench mortars figured prominently in the report.[18] The order to retreat was given too late. This setback was followed by others. Nine days later von Pappus reported on the situation at GHQSM to General von Hellingrath in Munich.

M. Kr. 1832

No. 17061   GHQSM   23.9.18

The atmosphere of OHL still remains very subdued and Excellency Ludendorff is in a nervous depression, which permits him to make no decisions. The OHL has not yet been able to give clear instructions to Army Sector A. The German success so triumphantly announced in yesterday's daily report is said to be considerably exaggerated.

In order to inform the OHL about conditions at the front, Colonel von Alberti, a Württemberger, is here, and has described with genuine Swabian frankness the situation as it actually is. Naturally it remains to be seen if he will be believed here. One can see and hear on all sides how much the respect for and trust in the OHL has been damaged.

How little the OHL is informed about the situation and how little they understand history can be seen from a remark the Field Marshal made to Colonel von Mertz in which he said that if Bavaria should receive Alsace, the Frankish provinces must naturally go to Prussia in exchange for this.

---

[18] M. Kr. 1832, no number, 14.9.18.

M. Kr. 1832

No. 17111   GHQSM   27.9.18

The American attacks between the Argonne and the Meuse fell
upon our only thinly held front; they succeeded in breaking through
beyond our main defense line and in gaining between two to four
kilometers of ground. With the help of our reserves, which had
already been brought up before the attack, the assault was brought
to a standstill on the following line: Montblainville, south of Montfauçon — and the bend of the Meuse by Vilosnes. The fighting continues. . . .

In conjunction with the French attacks, English and American
attacks began this morning south of the Arras-Cambrai road as far as
Gouzeaucourt and against the middle of the Second Army southeast
of Epehy.

M. Kr. 1832

No. 17131   GHQSM   28.9.18

[Attacks are reported all along the line.]

Further south between Epehy and Bellicourt additional enemy
attacks on a frontage of about 3½ divisions were directed against the
center of the Second Army. The attacks were carried out by American troops during which Tombois Ferme was lost; our counterattack
restored the previous situation and was pushed forward beyond
Lempire. . . .

The enemy continued his heavy attacks in the Champagne, in the
Argonne and on the Meuse. . . .

The American attack between Montblainville and the Meuse was
continued with the same intensity. Our opponent succeeded in forcing us back to Cièrges-Nantillois. For this reason we gave up Montfauçon, which was surrounded. Our front was withdrawn to Bri-
éulles sur Meuse. Again today in this whole sector fresh American
attacks are underway.

M. Kr. 1832

No. 17151   GHQSM   29.9.18

. . . Yesterday was a day of especially heavy fighting in the Champagne, . . . east of the Argonne the enemy had only limited local successes. Several of our divisions in the trenches were attacked by the French and the Americans up to six times. Squadrons of enemy airplanes often with a strength of up to 100 planes harassed our reserve divisions and our support troops in the rear areas. . . . Since early today fresh fighting is underway on the front of the 3rd Army in the region of Somme-Py and on that of the 5th Army east of the Argonne.

§ Von Pappùs wrote the following on the day Ludendorff admitted failure to the Crown Council.

M. Kr. 1832

No. 17159   GHQSM   29.9.18

Special Report

The questions which I posed today to Colonel von Mertz have brought the following response:

Our military situation in the West is very serious. In the 4th Army four trench divisions have lost all their artillery. During the attacks against the 17th Army proven divisions have failed. Our losses can no longer be made good by our reserves. The 7th Royal Saxon Division has lost all its officers. While we had committed our entire reserves to the main battlefronts at Cambrai, in the Champagne and the Argonne, heavy attacks, which were carried out only by the divisions in the trenches there and achieved a surprising success for the enemy, were launched at Ypres. Present conditions have made the OHL very dejected and the atmosphere here is apathetic. It is noteworthy that today in the regular briefing, which usually manages to transform our own setbacks into the greatest German victories, Captain Wewer began with these words: "Yesterday in Flanders our troops suffered a heavy defeat." This unaccustomed love of truth makes one think.

The Imperial Chancellor is here with Excellency von Hintze and there is at last some possibility that the OHL has honestly explained the actual situation on the Western Front to the civilian leaders of the Empire. The OHL has gone on too long and has missed the right time to tell the truth. Now the internal and external situation is so complicated that it has become very difficult to find a way out. The Political Section is said to have failed completely and to have pursued their own policy instead of informing the Foreign Office and giving them the essential information and directions according to which they should have been able to work. If they do not have the courage to tell the whole truth today a catastrophe will be unavoidable. The necessity of an armistice may now be for us only a question of weeks. We have lost 4,000 cannon in the last four weeks. . . .

I have received a very pessimistic report on the situation in the West from the Colonel von Mertz, who considers our present situation as extremely critical. The Foreign Office is completely aware of the gravity of the situation. The possible dismissal of the Chancellor and his entire staff was even considered today; Bernstorff, Solf and Bethmann have been mentioned as successors.

The severe fighting which has ended favorably for the 3rd and 5th Armies makes it still seem possible that our troops can hold out and that the reversal of the 4th Army was only a local failure and not a symptomatic phenomenon. The outcome of subsequent battles will certainly clarify this; they are underway again on all the main fighting fronts.

The only right thing to do is to stop concealing the seriousness of the situation from our homeland, so that our people will not be suddenly presented with facts which are too much for them to bear.

Telegram. No. 250 375

No. 1245   30/9/18   7:20 AM
Urgent: Bavarian War Minister, Munich.

Armistice and peace negotiations are to be initiated immediately. Hertling goes, Roedern substitute.

BAVARIAN MILITARY PLENIPOTENTIARY, GHQ, 29.8.18

§   The next day von Pappus again wrote a special report.

M. Kr. 1832

No. 17179   GHQSM   30.9.18

Special Report: Today at 11:50 AM the three military plenipotentiaries of the non-Prussian federal states were informed by Excellency Ludendorff in the presence of Colonel von Haye of the
following: . . . Rumania is restless and the Austrian southeast front
appears again to be threatened. These unfavorable conditions extend
to the Western Front where 22 divisions have been disbanded.
Enemy superiority has increased to between 30 and 40 divisions,
among which are 38 American divisions which are particularly
strong in manpower. The complement of our divisions has been
weakened appreciably and some are only remnants of divisions. In
addition to this, the masses of enemy tanks are becoming ever larger,
and our own ability to hold out against these mass tank attacks is
noticeably declining. Some of our divisions still show the greatest
courage and the same good old spirit and extraordinary bravery. . . .
Compared with these however, other divisions fail completely and
inevitably drag along their braver neighbors with them in their retreat. Where the cause of this is to be sought, if it is the result of a
shortage of officers or of other factors, cannot yet be clarified. The
Supreme Command no longer has the influence which is absolutely
necessary to coordinate the direction of operations. . . . In view of
these conditions, Field Marshal von Hindenburg and Excellency
Ludendorff have become convinced that in the interests of the German Army it was necessary to suspend hostilities and have reported
in this sense to His Majesty. Under these circumstances His Majesty has commanded the Imperial Chancellor and the Secretary of
State of the Foreign Office to undertake without further delay the
steps which are necessary.

The OHL's decision to make this frank report to His Majesty
concerning the actual military situation was not made emotionally. It
came much more as a result of the sad conviction that although the
splendid troops of the German Army were the equals of their enemy, they were no longer equal to the enemy machines, which in the
form of thousands of tanks now cause our line to totter. So much for
Excellency Ludendorff's information.

I have been informed from other sources that Excellency Ludendorff could not make up his mind to inform the appropriate au-

thorities about the facts of our military situation and to prepare a timely end to the difficult position in which we have found ourselves since the beginning of the retreat to the Siegfried position on 2.9.18. . . .

Only yesterday was His Majesty given a clear picture of our actual situation, and this was done at a time when it was too late.

The Emperor bore this difficult test with royal bearing and fortitude, but it would be a consolation and an encouragement to him if he found strong support among the federal princes. Perhaps it would be possible for His Majesty, the King, to send a dispatch to His Majesty, the Emperor, which would express the fact that our King stood by the side of the Emperor in these difficult hours.

M. Kr. 1832

No. 17191   GHQSM   1.10.18

. . . 3rd Army: The battles in the Champagne bore the character of ill coordinated attacks which lacked unity. . . . The enemy didn't notice that we had regained our position in the Argonne. Heavy American attacks on both sides of the Aire valley, whose aim has been Apremont and which lasted into the late evening, were repulsed by our perimeter defense. . . .

§   Von Pappus again announced important news:

M. Kr. 1832

Nr. 19195   GHQSM   1.10.18

Special Report: Confidential. Excellency Ludendorff urged the Foreign Office to issue the offer of peace immediately, if possible today, which, of course, is not possible. . . . they want the new government to take this step, because if it should be taken by the present government, there is reason to be concerned for internal peace and order. The reason for the OHL's urging is that they fear the troops can no longer hold out, because the reserves are almost completely exhausted. The OHL has assigned the guilt for the collapse of Bulgaria to the Foreign Office because they were unable to prevent an American chargé d'affaires from remaining in Sofia. The War Ministry is also being made to share the responsibility for the failure on the Western Front, because it failed to enforce the Law for the Support of the War sufficiently, with the result that too few troops were made available. . . .

His Majesty, the Emperor, goes to Potsdam today, the Chancellor returns to Berlin.

Von Payer is said to have refused the office of Chancellor and the candidacy of Prince Max of Baden appears to be likely.

M. Kr. 1832

No. 17211   GHQSM   2.10.18

. . . In the Army Group Gallwitz area we were able to improve our perimeter to a width of 3 km and a depth of 1 km at the expense of the Americans who dug in about 1 km behind our previous line.

No. 1 Secret   GHQSM   3.10.18

Special Report: [Von Köberle reported that Ludendorff had confirmed there was no hope for the German Army. Ludendorff told him that he had known this since August 8th, but had thought that the Army could hold out until winter. He no longer believes this is possible.] The enemy's superiority in men and machines is too great. The Americans have 39 divisions in France, which have twice the infantry strength of a German division. . . .

The German people will discover too late how false their hopes for a negotiated peace were. The peace will be very hard and pitiless. . . .

The collapse of Bulgaria is not really inconvenient for the OHL, for it serves to conceal the admission of our own collapse, whose approach they themselves for far too long a time, indeed until 14 days ago, did not want to admit. This failure to recognize our own situation undoubtedly had a negative affect upon the measures taken by the OHL. Fourteen days ago today they told Czar Ferdinand that it was impossible to send him troops to support him and today they want to ship five divisions to Serbia and Bulgaria, despite the further worsening of the situation in the Western Theater of Operations. Since [20.9.18] the actions of the OHL have lacked any systematic purpose and reveal no overall plan.

Telegram No. 255 645

No. 187   GHQSM   5.10.18 12:40 PM
                Royal Bavarian War Minister, Munich.

Personal. Today at 1:00 AM the peace note was sent to Bern. It can hardly be in America before Monday, therefore strictest secrecy necessary. The Czar (of Bulgaria) has abdicated.
                    BAVARIAN MILITARY PLENIPOTENTIARY

M. Kr. 1832

No. 17251   GHQSM   4.10.8
    [Attacks made north of Somme-Py were beaten back.]
    East of the Argonne heavy enemy movement continues and the expected attack began today.

§ The American attack in the Meuse-Argonne sector caused Colonel Holland to send a detailed report to the Württemberg Minister of War.

Personal Affairs of the Württemberg War Minister, Vol. 104

                    The Meuse-Argonne   5.10.18

    . . . Our troops have had to endure particularly heavy attacks on the western edge of the Argonne and in the area between the Argonne and the Meuse. The Americans attacked, employing fresh divisions in exceptionally thick masses from early morning until the evening. On the Aire they were able to push forward as far as Fleville and Exermort. In the counterattack at Fleville, the rear area trenches to the south of it, and Exermont were retaken. Elsewhere the attacks failed with exceptionally high enemy losses and the Americans suffered a severe defeat. So far today only light action is reported from the Champagne and the battlefields east of the Argonne.

§   The British and the French view of American fighting qualities differed somewhat from that of the Germans, as the following report, which covered the fighting between September 12 and October 18 reveals.

WO 106/528/8701

Notes on American Offensive Operations
(From information received from French sources)
Secret

St. Mihiel Offensive of September 12th.

The date originally fixed for the attack had to be postponed for ten days owing to the American preparations being belated. The attack was carried out by the American 1st Army, under the command of General Pershing, consisting of eight American divisions on the southern flank of the salient, one French and one American Division on the Northern flank, between these two attacks there were three French Divisions, while opposed to them were 7 German and 2 Austrian Divisions. The French lent a large amount of artillery, aeroplanes, tanks, Staff Officers, etc., and helped in the preliminary organisation.

The attack took place under exceptionally favourable conditions on the 12th, as it caught the enemy halfway through his arrangements for evacuating, which should have been completed on the 15th. The bombardment did not cut the wire and the Americans had to stamp it down or cut it by hand. Fortunately there was practically no resistance, as is shown by the fact that the total killed was under 200, whilst one French Division took 2,500 prisoners and had only 4 men killed. It was hoped that the two enemy Divisions in the point of the salient would have been cut off, but they got away by a new road through the forest apparently without any great difficulty.

The American attack from the South reached the neighbourhood of Vigneulles just about the same time as the Northern attack was approaching it, and the two appear to have engaged each other, both reporting that they could not get on on account of intense machine-gun fire. After the initial attack the Germans appear to have got clear away, owing to the great confusion existing in the American lines on the communications leading to the front, and though it was reported that there was great confusion also behind the German lines, no effort could be made to exploit the success.

Generally speaking, the set-piece part of the operations was satisfactorily organised and carried out, particularly the approach march and the concentration of the guns, but the army was immobilised after the first twelve hours by inexperience in re-organising under battle conditions. A serious feature, also, was that a large amount of rolling stock was locked up behind the American Army, and although urgently required elsewhere, it could not be extricated. But perhaps the most unfortunate part of an otherwise successful operation was that it confirmed the American High Command in an exaggerated estimate of the efficiency of the American military machine, — and of their ability to control it.

This has been dearly paid for since.

Attack in the Argonne — commencing September 26th, 1918.

The American Divisions taking part were in many cases quite raw. The objectives were ambitious, and had they been reached the results would have been almost, if not quite, decisive. This attack was commenced on a frontage of 30 kilometres in conjunction with a French attack further West. The initial arrangements appear to have been well carried out, a large number of French Staff Officers etc. assisting. The assault was launched in a fog, and the enemy, who had previously withdrawn his artillery, put up very little resistance in the forward areas. There was practically no enemy shelling and such resistance as was met with was mainly from machine gun pockets, which in some cases were over-run and not properly mopped up, and gave a good deal of trouble later.

On the first day the Americans advanced about 11 kilometres, but did not maintain all their ground. The following days were characterized by confusion everywhere. The American idea of road control appeared to be that someone on the spot would rise to the occasion and straighten things out. In actual practice this led to one unit's transport trying to jockey that of every other unit. The result was great congestion on the roads on which transport was often double-banked, effectively blocking them for hours at a time. Small bodies of American troops were scattered everywhere, not apparently under any control. Where work was being carried out three men appeared to be trying to do one man's job; lorries were seen covered with soldiers who ought to have been walking, and supplies were being looted from supply columns as they went forward. The result was that the soldiers in the front line were unable to get either food or ammunition. Requests for reinforcements coming in from the front, which were usually granted, still further added to the congestion, and when supplies did not arrive parties began to drift to the rear, and effectives melted. Liaison from rear to front appeared to be unsatisfactory, and panicky reports kept coming in, such as might be expected in the case of raw troops, as indeed these were. Liaison between divisions was also insufficient, and one division frequently did not know where those on its flank were. All this time Army Headquarters were making frenzied endeavours to get the troops forward, but the knowledge and grip of the situation necessary to organise attacks in these conditions were not possessed by the Staff. Orders for operations were issued by Army Headquarters, which reached the troops too late to be acted upon, and only added to the confusion.

The net result of all this was that from the 27th September to the 18th October the Army only gained another 5 kilometres, whilst wastage from wounds, sickness and straggling was very severe. On one occasion a division moving up in support had 5,000 casualties from enemy artillery without firing a shot. Efforts made to establish order behind the battle field have only been partially successful, discipline is weak, and men on road control apparently found it necessary to use their revolvers – a method unheard of in the French Army.

From the 26th September to the 18th October, 17 American Divisions were employed, equivalent in strength to over 30 of the French, British or German divisions. These 17 divisions engaged 23 weak and tired enemy divisions and at the cost of heavy losses effected very little. American divisions in General Gouraud's Army, where they have had a fair chance, have done splendidly, and it is believed that the same applies to the divisions with the British, and these few divisions have probably taken more prisoners recently than all the rest of the American Army put together.

The general impression is that, in spite of the gallantry and spirit of the individual, and owing to inexperience, particularly in the higher ranks, American divisions employed in large blocks under their own command, suffer wastage out of all proportion to results achieved, and generally do not pull more than a small fraction of their weight.

It is felt that in insisting on the premature formation of large American Armies, General Pershing has not interpreted the altruistic wishes of the American Nation, and that he has incurred a grave responsibility both as regards unnecessary loss of life amongst his troops, and in the failure of the operations.

Copy of Letter from General Du Cane No. 724 of 19.10.18 to C.I.G.S.

I saw to-day the American Representative with MARSHAL FOCH, Colonel BENTLEY-MOTT. He has just returned from a visit to the American front on the MEUSE.

He told me that the fighting has been severe recently, and that the casualties have been heavy. General PERSHING told him a day or two ago that the battle casualties since 25th September amounted to 80,000. In addition the American troops are suffering much from sickness, the most prevalent diseases being pneumonia, diarrhoea and dysentery. The American troops are evidently not acclimatized and suffer acutely from the cold and wet. Their troubles in this respect are no doubt aggravated by faulty administration.

It appears that General PERSHING has given up attacking on a broad front, as his losses were so heavy for the results obtained. Each of his operations is now conducted on the front of 1 division and he considers that he has achieved a considerable amount of success in attracting counter-attacks, wherever he has gained ground, in which he has inflicted very heavy losses on the enemy.

General PERSHING estimates that he has engaged 27 German Divisions on the MEUSE front and he considers that he has very materially assisted operations elsewhere by attracting this force to the American front in order to protect the vital objectives of the BRIEY mines and the MEZIERES-MONTMEDY railway. He will continue his operations in this area irrespective of losses as long as Marshal FOCH considers it necessary to do so.

Four Divisions recently landed have now been broken up to replace losses in the remainder. It is clear that wastage was under-estimated and insufficient reinforcements have been provided.

Colonel MOTT also said that 10 Divisional Artilleries are without horses. I understand that a request for assistance in the matter of horses has been addressed to Marshal FOCH, and it is probable that the Americans are casting covetous eyes on the British reserves of horses, which they think exist.

(Sd.) J. P. DU CANE
Lieut.-General, British Military Representative,
with Marshal C.-in-C., Allied Forces.

19.10.19.

§   The Bavarians continued the story.

M. Kr. 1832

No. 17281   GHQSM   6.10.18

[The Franco-American attack continues at Somme-Py.]

Captured orders of the 2nd American Infantry Division, which is fighting there, and is supposed to be one of the best American assault divisions, indicate that this division is expected to decide the offensive on this crucial wing. In the opinion of the German troops opposite them, the individual American soldier is very brave but the troops as a whole lack a sense of unity and consequently their attacks break up quickly. . . . For three days now in the Argonne behind the left wing of the 3rd Army a pocket of Americans consisting of about 600 men has been holding out and has not yet been overcome despite the very heavy losses which it has suffered. Today a flamethrower attack is going to be made against this detachment. Enemy pilots, who are supposed to bring these people food and ammunition, have dropped them into our lines. . . .

No. 8 Secret   GHQSM   7.10.18

Special Report: [Von Köberle says Hindenburg believes that only an honorable peace can be accepted.]

I have the impression however, that in many cases the gentlemen of OHL simply do not realize what the enemy will demand in terms of military security, if they agree at all to negotiations, which is likely. Meanwhile the officers chosen for the armistice negotiation, headed by Excellency von Gündell, are sitting with bags packed ready to depart.

As far as the internal political situation is concerned one frequently hears the opinion expressed that it is a good thing the Left Wing parties must take the odium upon themselves for the conclusion of peace. The storm of popular indignation will then turn against these parties.

They hope later to climb back into the saddle and to continue governing according to the old formula.

M. Kr. 1832

No. 17321   GHQSM   8.10.18

. . . Very heavy American attacks on both sides of the Aire Valley against the heights of Chatel led to the loss of this place and of the northern heights.

No. 13 Secret   GHQSM   12.10.18

[Von Köberle had been asked to be careful about what he says, so

that the enemy doesn't get an idea of how bad the German situation
is.]

In Berlin the frank presentation of our military situation has
produced a kind of panic in a segment of the people's representatives
which has then spilled over into wider circles. [Ludendorff has
reported that between April and September 40 fresh divisions have
been added to the Allied strength.] . . . of the enemy divisions the
American divisions have a battalion strength of a thousand men, the
English of 750, the French of 560, ours of only 500 to 450; in fact
12 divisions have no more than 200 per battalion. We have broken
up 23 and now must reduce the regiments to two battalions, and the
battalions to three companies, in order to avoid further dis-
bandments. . . . [Ludendorff said that after Cambrai the troops had
learned not to be afraid of tanks.] . . . But the 18.7. and 8.8. of this
year have shown that they are able to cause panic even among
seasoned troops, particularly when favored by mist and in masses, as
they now appear. Consequently the High Command cannot be at all
sure that they can depend upon the troops' power of resistance. In
the face of the masses which now appear our artillery is not numerous enough to prevent, along with its other tasks, a tank breakthrough. The tanks which have broken through then employ machine
guns with which they attack our infantry from the rear, which has a
negative affect upon morale.

Americans: Our estimate concerning the number of Americans
who had arrived in Europe was correct until the end of March. From
then on the Entente, by putting aside all other shipments, trans-
ported 250,000 men monthly, so that there are now 39 divisions in
France.

The Americans are not yet very well trained and led, but they are
personally brave and tough and their nerves have not yet been
exhausted. In the attacks west of the Meuse, they continued to
advance in closely packed columns, unmoved by the artillery fire
employed against them and as a result made a great dent in our thin
lines through which by means of their numbers they were ultimately
able to break.

A careful consideration of the situation reveals that if we do not
wish to place our army in danger of complete destruction during the
months of October and November, we must seek as quickly as
possible an armistice and peace.

§   The preparation of the home front for the news of Germany's defeat.

Nachlass Conrad Haussmann Fasz. 22 Hauptstaatsarchiv Stuttgart

Secret. Only for official use
Zu. R. Pr. No. 1016/18.P.   BERLIN, 11 October 1918

[This was an instruction issued by the Chief of the Reich's Press Bureau to the leading newspapers.]

The German government's answer to the questions posed by Wilson after the receipt of our peace note is primarily conditioned by the military situation.

According to the carefully considered judgment of the Supreme Command this situation is that the continuation of the war offers the enemy an ever-increasing opportunity to make use of his superiority. The enemy continually receives large reinforcements from America with which our reserves of men and material cannot keep pace. The longer we must fight, especially on the decisive, widely extended Western Front, the more the situation changes to our disadvantage. To this must be added the fact that one of our allies has already completely collapsed and that it is only a question of time until both our remaining allies will breathe their last.

We must face this fact squarely, because any deception and optimism would only increase the danger which threatens us. . . .

For these reasons the new German government, in compliance with the urgent request of the Supreme Command, has decided in favor of a decisive step towards peace. . . .

The American President's questions leave no doubt that our enemies are completely aware of the advantage of their situation. Therefore we are confronted with the bitter necessity of showing much greater willingness to oblige in our reply than will be comprehensible to German public opinion which until now has had hopes which were in part greatly exaggerated. It is now up to our press to handle the German government's reply in such a way that it prevents the collapse of the will to resist on the home front and among the fighting troops. . . .

. . . in view of the situation in which we now find ourselves, we must encourage the President to negotiate and through him influence his allies in favor of greater moderation. If we fail, then the last chance to achieve a negotiated peace which would be more or less worth signing will have been finally missed. The result of the war would in this case be a peace which the enemy would dictate to us.

But if we pursue the proper middle course between despondency and overconfidence, then we are completely justified in the hope that it will be possible, with the help of the yet unbroken military strength of our army and navy and through a policy which has the trust of the people, to achieve a peace which is worthy of Germany and satisfies our honor. The Government as well as the Supreme Command understand that in giving this answer to Wilson's queries the question of Alsace-Lorraine and Poland are recognized as international problems. It is sad that we had to decide to do this but it could not be avoided if the task of gaining peace were not to fail.

Naturally the recognition of the international character of both questions does not mean that we wish to give up portions of Prussia which have a Polish population and Alsace-Lorraine. Wilson certainly does not expect this of us, or he would have expressed himself accordingly in his statements. The settlement of the Polish and Alsace-Lorraine question will be made when we negotiate peace. . . .

The final question of the President is easy to answer. We now have a popular parliamentary government. The Imperial Chancellor has spoken in their name and in that of the great majority of the Reichstag, and thus in the name of the people. Wilson can be satisfied with this and he will indeed be satisfied, especially if we do not annoy him by references to his self-righteousness. It is known that he follows our press very carefully.

According to what has been said above the situation must indeed be viewed as serious but in no way as directly threatening or even hopeless.

The ability and determination of the people to fight on longer in case of necessity requires particular stress.

Between 1916 and 1918 the German forces on the Western Front were reorganized into Army Groups which were commanded by the German Crown Prince, Prince Ruppert of Bavaria, and Duke Albert of Württemberg. The War Diary of

Duke Albert's Army Group provides glimpses of the Americans during 1918. Duke Albert's Group of armies occupied the trenches from the positions around Verdun to the Swiss border. During the final months of the war the presence of the Americans became a growing problem for Duke Albert's staff. An attack on the Lorraine Front by the Americans might well have broken the German line and opened the way for the Allies to outflank the entire German position on the Western Front.[19] The attack never took place but the fear that it would was an ever-present factor in the thinking of the German High Command. The following excerpts are from the War Diary in the *Heeresarchiv,* Stuttgart.

10.8.1918 . . . Situation report: . . . Apparently the enemy intends to garrison the Lorraine front entirely with American troops. . . .

28.9.1918 . . . Situation report: . . . In view of the way in which the trenches are manned, which is known to OHL, and the ever diminishing reserves behind the Front, consisting for the most part of already battle weary troops, the situation here must be characterized as very precarious. . . .

12.10.1918. Weekly report about the enemy position: The Army Group's view of the situation:

The numerous divisions which the enemy still has at his disposal enable him to launch an offensive against our front at any time, without suspending his successful attacks upon the Army Groups, Crown Prince Ruppert and German Crown Prince. As his experience in Flanders shows, he need only slightly reinforce his front line divisions to do this. The obvious advantage of occupying German territory if possible, and of influencing Alsace-Lorraine at the same time politically, before the beginning of peace negotiations could cause the enemy to move at any time from a state of preparation for an offensive to an offensive itself.

Although no signs of an immediately impending offensive are to be discerned, the ample provision of the enemy trenches with depots

---

[19] Kielmanscgg, 659.

for troops and munitions, the enlargement of several airports, and the expansion of the enemy communications network, opposite the left half of the 19th Army front and the right half of Army Sector A's position deserve particular attention. The closest surveillance of the distribution of enemy strength is called for here and the army has ordered the necessary steps to be taken. Due to our almost complete lack of reserves, the situation on the Lorraine Front must be described as very uncertain.

9.11.18 . . . the possibility of an enemy attack on the Lorraine Front cannot be dismissed. . . .

11.11.18. A brief description of the "incidents" in Strasbourg.

After smaller gatherings, which were accompanied by only minor incidents, had taken place on the evenings of the 7th and 8th of November, a mob of pugnacious young people of both sexes collected at the Brant-Platz during the evening of the 9th of November. Only a few soldiers were present. Toward midnight the mob, shouting wildly, gathered before the house of the local commandant, Major Schmitt, in the Ruprechtsauer Allee. Without meeting much resistance, the crowd forced their way into the building and plundered the dwelling of everything that could easily be carried away. Towards 1 o'clock the approach of an armored car which was stationed nearby in the Ruprechtsauer Allee drove away the mob. The rest of the night passed quietly.

In the early morning of the 10th of November a Worker's and Soldier's Council was formed in Strasbourg which, as soon as it was in possession of the station and the main guard house, issued orders and entrusted its agents with their execution. In this way for example they provided for the maintenance of order in the streets by their own patrols. The council confiscated several military vehicles for this purpose; all military personnel in the streets, officers as well as men, were stopped by soldiers with red badges, who took from them by force if there was any resistance weapons, cockades, epaulettes, and tabs.

In order to maintain security and order in the area around the Ruprechtsauer Allee, the Army Group also organized street patrols in the afternoon of 10.11. Machine guns were set up in the telephone exchange and the General Staff Building, in order to defend these buildings.

At 5:30 in the afternoon a delegation of the Worker's and Soldier's Council appeared at the General Staff Building led by an NCO with a red flag and demanded the surrender of the weapons which were there. By means of friendly negotiation the Ia, Major von Stülpnagel, arranged that the weapons were to remain in the house and that the Worker's and Soldier's Council would mount a guard of six men to be stationed in the building to protect it. The night of the 10th–11th passed quietly.

. . . On the 11.11.1918 at 11:55 AM German time the armistice agreed upon with the Entente began. . . .

12.11.18. The behavior of the Civil Population:

West of the Rhine it was generally hostile, especially in the cities. Batteries of the k.u.k. artillery in the area of Army Sector A had their guns taken away from them by the populace. In several places there were shooting incidents between the populace and the military. . . .

§   The War Diary of the XIII Army Corps told a similar story.

9.11.18   HQ Norroy

[The enemy attack began at 11:00 AM. German forces in Sector B were particularly hard hit.]

The enemy succeeded in penetrating the perimeter only in the left-hand trenches of [Sector] B which were held by the 18th Bavarian Infantry Regiment.

Here, during course of the battle he was able to advance beyond the main line of resistance [H.W.L.] A counterattack brought him to a halt northeast of the black Haag. Elsewhere the main line of resistance was held. Several times the enemy infantry attempted to contact our line by waving.

Our artillery played a magnificent part in the repulse of the enemy assaults. During the afternoon probing attacks by strong hostile patrols also took place. . . .

Reports from home have stated, that Soldier's Councils have seized executive power in Kiel, the Hansa cities, Hanover, and Cologne. Representatives of these people also arrived in the reserve area, the fortresses Metz and Diedenhofen, and interrupted the orderly movement of supplies which at this time was vitally necessary.

As a result of this interference there was a shortage of rolling stock urgently needed to remove material that was to be evacuated. An order was received on the same day from OHL to set up advisory councils to provide a liaison between officers and men, in order to deepen mutual trust, and to make possible cooperation during the difficult tasks of retirement and demobilization.

CHAPTER VII

The Return Home to "Normalcy"

§ There really was not much more to say. Brigadier General
Wagstaff complained that the American Army of Occupation
in Germany was too friendly with the enemy.

There is a good deal too much friendly feeling between the Americans and the Germans. . . . The Germans are charging the Americans whatever they like and the Americans pay.[1]

He also hoped that the Americans would be impressed by
and learn from the British Army of Occupation.[2] It was a
false hope.

The news from the United States was not too encouraging.
Mr. Hughes attacked "the extent to which government control of private enterprise had grown during the war." Colville
Barclay told his government that the Republican Party would
now "direct its energies . . . towards giving a freer scope to
private enterprise."[3] Even before that the Anglo-American
Breweries had appealed to the British government for some
kind of protection against the threat of Prohibition in America, which would ruin the British shareholders. There was
nothing the government could do.[4] Then the news came that

---

[1] W.O. 106/499 A, Dec. 10 to D.M.O.
[2] W.O. 106/499 A, Dec. 16 to D.M.O.
[3] F.O. 371/3493/7871
[4] F.O. 371/3431/7867

the United States Senate resented the fact that Wilson had not consulted them about his policy toward the League of Nations.[5] America was returning to normalcy.

Germany was left to sign the Versailles Treaty or, as the Germans like to call it, "Diktat." General Groener, who had taken Ludendorff's place, had been forced to say that the nation was not capable of resuming the war and should sign. Germany was left shorn of the old symbols which had represented an ordered society and around which loyalties had been built. The New Republic brought with it only the symbol, but really not the responsibility, for defeat. Germany sought other symbols.

F.O. 371/3493/7871

No. 1071   BRITISH EMBASSY, WASHINGTON, December 4, 1918

SIR,

I have the honour to transmit herewith extracts from the "New York Times" containing the text of a speech by Mr. Hughes in which he condemned the extent to which Government control of private enterprises had grown during the war.

He stated that all government enterprises tend to inefficiency and deprecated the continued operation by the Government of the railways and the telegraph system. He also pointed out that antitrust laws should not operate against large businesses simply on account of their size, but should provide such supervision as is necessary to ensure that the great power wielded by such concerns is not wrongly used.

The speech indicates once more that the Republican party will direct its energies towards opposing the government control of public utilities and towards giving a freer scope to private enterprise.

I have the honor to be, with the highest respect, Sir, your most obedient, humble servant,

COLVILLE BARCLAY

The Right Honourable A. J. Balfour, O.M., M.P.

-----

[5] F.O. 371/3493/7871

F.O. 371/3431/7867

62, Broad Street Avenue, London, E. C. 2
15 November, 1918

To the Rt. Hon. Arthur J. Balfour, M.P.,
Secretary of State for Foreign Affairs.

SIR,

On behalf of British Shareholders in Anglo-American Brewery Companies we desire to submit the following statement for your earnest consideration:

In consequence of a widespread agitation amongst a certain section of the community in favour of total prohibition, the brewing industry in the various States of North America has been from time to time threatened with total extinction.

About five and twenty to thirty years ago a number of American breweries were sold to English companies at high prices and the capital stock of these concerns is mainly held by British shareholders.

At the present time there are about twelve or fourteen Anglo-American Brewing Companies, the principal ones being the following: —

The Bartholomay Brewing Co., (of Rochester)	New York
The Chicago Brewing Company	Chicago
The City of Chicago Brewing & Malting Co., Ltd.	Chicago
The Denver United Breweries Limited	Denver, Colo.
Goebel Brewing Company	Detroit, Mich.
Indianapolis Brewing Company	Indiana
Frank Jones Brewing Company	New Hampshire
Milwaukee and Chicago Breweries Limited	Milwaukee and Chicago
New England Breweries	New Jersey & Boston
New York Breweries	New York
St. Louis Breweries	St. Louis
San Francisco Breweries	California

The total share and debenture capital of these Companies amounts to over twelve million pounds sterling; they are all registered in England and their capital stocks *duly quoted in the official list of the London Stock Exchange.*

As a direct result of the agitation of the prohibitionists four of the above named companies viz., The Denver United Breweries, The

Goebel Brewing Company, the Indianapolis and the Frank Jones
have already had to cease brewing alcoholic liquors and their businesses have been practically ruined — with the consequent financial
loss to the shareholders. This state of things has been brought about
by State Legislation and no compensation has been paid to the
companies affected.

Having failed to carry other States with them in the direction of
enforced temperance the prohibitionists have of late been en-
deavouring to induce the Federal Government to take powers to
have total prohibition in the whole of the States. The War has given
these people an opportunity, of which they have not been slow to
avail themselves, to press their views, and from being purely a
matter of a grievance against particular States, the Anglo-American
Breweries are now faced with the threat of Federal Government
interference, and as a War measure the brewing of any alcoholic
beverage is absolutely prohibited as from the 30th of November
instant.

The position thus created has naturally caused great anxiety to the
Boards of the various Companies and at a recent conference of
representatives of the Boards it was decided to make representations
to the British Foreign Office pointing out the seriousness of the
situation as affecting the interests of British shareholders and ex-
pressing the hope that the Foreign Office would see their way to
bring the matter before the Government of the United States.

The British Shareholders do not for a moment wish to challenge
the right of the Electors or Legislatures of the U.S.A. to decide
whether beer or other alcoholic liquors shall be permitted to be
manufactured or consumed in their respective States, but they do
question and challenge their moral right to destroy those businesses
which have been created and developed under the direct sanction of
their laws without giving and making adequate compensation to
those who have invested their capital in the Brewing industries with
the full and reasonable expectation that their property and vested
interests were just as safe secure and sacred as any other kind of
property or vested interest.

The undersigned recognising and appreciating the close relationship now happily existing between the peoples of both countries
sincerely hope that this matter may be discussed in a friendly spirit

and that some equitable settlement may be arrived at which will remove from the thousands of people in this country who have invested their money in the Anglo-American Breweries the feeling that they have been unfairly treated and impoverished.

In this hope and trust we humbly beg you to have the facts duly transmitted through the proper channels to the authorities at Washington, and trust you will see your way to give our appeal your support.

We beg to remain, Sir. Your obedient servants.

F.O. 371/3431/7867

FOREIGN OFFICE, S.W. 1., December 2nd, 1918

SIR: —

I have to transmit to you herewith a copy of a letter received from Mr. H. A. Kidd regarding the position of Anglo-American Breweries in the United States under the new legislation introduced by the Federal Government concerning alcoholic beverages.

In point of law, there would not appear to be any valid grounds of complaint on the part of British Companies in the brewing trade in the United States if they receive the same treatment as American Companies engaged in that business. The enclosed letter does not suggest that there has been or is likely to be any discrimination in the treatment of foreign Companies. If "prohibition" becomes the law throughout the United States and no compensation is given to American citizens engaged in the prohibited trade, there would appear to be no ground on which His Majesty's Government could ask for compensation to British Subjects and any such request might not only be refused but might be also resented.

I request that you will ascertain from the United States Government what measures have so far been taken and what further steps are contemplated and furnish me with a report.

I am with great truth, Sir, Your most obedient, humble Servant,

(For the Secretary of State)
(Signed) VICTOR WELLESLEY

F.O. 371/3493/7871

United States of America
Decypher. Mr. Barclay (Washington) December 19th. 1918
No. 5594.   R. 1.40. P.M. December 20th. 1918

Debate took place in the Senate yesterday on the resolution proposed by Senator Knox.

Resolutions proposed indefinite postponement of questions of League of Nations and Freedom of Seas.

Resolutions will probably be discussed again at the end of the week.

Situation as regards the sentiment on League of Nations is obscure. No political party alignment has yet taken place but there is a feeling of resentment common to both parties that Senate has not been consulted and that country has been left in the dark. Contradictory articles appear constantly in the press based on vague rumours from Paris. No serious notice should however be taken of them. Public sentiment has not yet crystallised and is not likely to do so until question of League of Nations with obligations and responsibilities attendant on it has been put clearly before the people.

Further debates on resolutions may throw some light on the sentiments of the Senate though I learn on reliable authority that no definite attitude will or can be adopted until some clear pronouncement is made in Paris.

BOOK MANUFACTURE

Over There: European Reaction to Americans in World War I was composed by Allied Typesetting Company, Dexter, Michigan. Printing and binding were by NAPCO Graphic Arts, Inc., Milwaukee, Wisconsin. The internal design was by the F. E. Peacock Publishers, Inc. art department. Evelyn Hansen designed the cover. The type is Times Roman.